CAPITALIST REVOLUTIONARY

JOHN MAYNARD KEYNES

Roger E. Backhouse
Bradley W. Bateman

HARVARD UNIVERSITY PRESS
Cambridge, Massachusetts
London, England
2011

Printed in the United States of America

Library of Congress Cataloging-in-Publication Data
Backhouse, Roger, 1951–
Capitalist revolutionary : John Maynard Keynes / Roger E. Backhouse,
Bradley W. Bateman.
p. cm.
Includes bibliographical references and index.
ISBN 978-0-674-05775-3 (alk. paper)
1. Keynes, John Maynard, 1883–1946. 2. Keynesian economics.
I. Bateman, Bradley W., 1956– II. Title.
HB103.K47B25 2011
330.15'6092—dc22 2011010437

To our families, past, present, and future

CONTENTS

CAPITALIST REVOLUTIONARY

1

KEYNES RETURNS, BUT WHICH KEYNES?

Following the financial crisis of September 2008 when the American investment bank Lehman Brothers collapsed, threatening to engulf the entire banking system, the British economist John Maynard Keynes returned to center stage. In the popular press and in the writings of many economists, Keynes featured prominently as governments around the world urgently sought ways to avoid economic collapse. In the United States, the *New York Times* contained articles titled "What would Keynes have done?" (October 28, 2008), "The old economist, relevant amid the rubble" (September 18, 2009), and "An old master back in fashion" (November 1, 2009). Likewise, in Britain the *Financial Times* ran pieces titled "The undeniable shift to Keynes" (December 29, 2008) and "In the long run we are all dependent on Keynes" (January 7, 2009). In France, *Le Monde* talked of "The revenge of Keynes" (October 2, 2008). After only a brief delay, critics of Keynes's ideas also began to appear; but the emergence of such critics only served to emphasize the fact of his return, for only a few years earlier Keynes's name would not even have appeared in public debate about economic policy: his ideas were seen as having so little relevance that it did not even seem necessary to mention his name when discussing the performance of the economy.

As the threat of another Great Depression receded, and bank bailouts caused a surge in government borrowing, Keynes became more controversial. Attention shifted to public-sector debt, and hence to the relationship between China and the United States, as well as to the problems of the weaker Eurozone countries (Greece, Portugal, and Spain), where economic stability was threatened by the possibility that they might default on their debts and that interest rates might spiral out of control. Even in countries where there was little risk of the government's defaulting on its debt, there was widely perceived to be a need for spending cuts to urgently reduce budget deficits. Only a year and a half after the financial crisis, Keynes was seen by many as a luxury that countries with high budget deficits could not afford.

However, the Keynes who was recently and so suddenly resurrected is far from being the only Keynes to have appeared in public debate in the last half-century. He is not the same person who was famous in the middle of the twentieth century, during what was widely called "the age of Keynes." Neither is he the Keynes who was rejected so decisively by economists and politicians in the 1970s. Keynes and Keynesianism have been reinterpreted time and time again, both by those who seek to claim his authority for positions they want to adopt and by those who denounce him, using him as a foil against which they can present their own ideas. This repeated reinterpretation should not be a surprise. We now see the world differently from the way people saw it in the 1940s, in the immediate aftermath of the Second World War; in the 1960s, when Kennedy and Johnson were trying to manage the economy; or even in the 1970s, when the current movements against "big government" and the welfare state were first getting under way.

One reason for seeing Keynes differently is that the world has changed. The trends that get swept into the category of "globalization" have transformed the world economy, just as the end of the Cold War and the end of Communism transformed the political climate. Present-day skepticism about whether politicians and businessmen can be trusted to do anything other than line their own pockets contrasts dramatically with the widespread confidence in government and planning found in the thirty years following the Second World War. These changes have had a profound effect on which Keynes people have been able to see.

There is, however, another reason for seeing Keynes differently. As we will show in the following chapters, Keynes and Keynesianism were multidimensional. Unusually, Keynes straddled the worlds of academia, journalism, government, and business, with the result that he cannot (or should not) be pigeonholed only as the designer of economic policies or just as an important economic theorist who sought the fundamental laws governing the operation of capitalist economies. He was both of these, and to leave out one or the other of them distorts our view of the whole. He was, moreover, also a philosopher who offered a moral critique of capitalism.

Keynes the Designer of Economic Policy

In the thirty years after the Second World War, Keynes was widely seen as the architect of the postwar prosperity that was so dramatically lifting living standards in the industrial democracies. The popular idea of his work, promoted by many academic economists, was that Keynes had devised a system of economic policymaking that made it possible to fine-tune the economy with careful adjustments of fiscal policy. If the economy threatened to fall into recession, government spending would be increased, or taxes reduced by just enough to maintain full employment, and if it threatened to overheat, these policies would go into reverse. The "New Economics," a term that became widely used to describe Keynesian ideas in the 1940s, was argued by many to provide a simple toolkit for engineering stable economic growth. With the right people at the wheel, the economy could be "steered" toward the desired outcomes of high employment and low inflation.

Today, that postwar vision of steady economic growth caused by finely tuned adjustments to fiscal policy has been largely forgotten. The remarkable period of stability around the millennium, often called the "great moderation" after Federal Reserve chair Ben Bernanke popularized the term, was widely attributed to well-designed monetary policy and the abandonment of fiscal fine-tuning. The ambitions of those looking to Keynes for solutions to the 2008 crisis were therefore very different. They turned to him not as the architect of stable economic growth but as the economist who knew how to prevent the meltdown of the financial system from tipping the world into another Great Depression. In the autumn of 2008, people were searching for tools to use in an emergency, not a comfortable steering wheel that could be used to guide the economy on a smooth path of full employment.

Though people have recently questioned whether free markets are the panacea that they had been thought to be in the 1990s and 2000s, few of those who invoked Keynes after the financial crisis of 2008 were dreaming about a return to an idyllic world of well-balanced economic growth driven by carefully planned economic policy. They were not calling on the same Keynes that President John F. Kennedy's advisers had called on fifty years earlier. Those calling on him in 1960 genuinely believed in economic management, as a sort of social engineering, and they did so with a degree of self-confidence that it is hard to imagine today. In the same way that Kennedy's successor, President Lyndon Johnson, instituted a Great Society Program and a War on Poverty, they wanted to use Keynesian policies to achieve their vision of a stable, well-managed economy growing smoothly into the future. American capitalism was thought to be successful because scientific management had transformed American business, but there was still a fear that it was losing the technological race with the Soviet Union. "Scientific" planning could be used to promote economic growth, and the fruits of economic growth could also be used to make sure that the unemployed and the poor did not get left behind. In contrast, those calling on Keynes in 2008 were confronted with the possibility that the capitalist system might collapse, and were desperate to find a solution.

Logically, of course, these two different visions of Keynes do not have to be mutually exclusive. One could build a theory of the economy that provides both a guide to righting the economy when it slips into crisis and a framework for managing it well during more normal times. From the Second World War to the 1960s, Keynesianism rested on a vision of planning, designed by experts, using the latest scientific methods. That vision was a far cry from today's world, in which there is widespread skepticism about whether government can do anything efficiently, in which government services are routinely subcontracted to private companies, and in which corporations, many of them transnational, populate a world of casino capitalism in which speculation and irresponsible investor behavior can tank the economy. The Keynes being resurrected today is thus a different Keynes from the one who was on center stage fifty years ago. There would seem to be a Keynes for good times and a Keynes for bad times. Even in the short period since the 2008 crisis, people have sought different things from Keynes. Initially, the main thing they wanted was a way to avoid catastrophe. But as the dust cleared, it became more important to understand why financial capitalism could suddenly and unexpectedly collapse. After thirty years of free-market ideology and rising living standards, they wanted to know why this system could deliver such a terrible crisis. This search required a different Keynes.

Keynes the Economic Theorist

The Keynes of the popular imagination is the designer of economic policy, whether policies to avert catastrophe or policies to fine-tune the economy. However, behind this Keynes lies the economist, much more visible to other economists, who created a new way of analyzing capitalist economies. His great book, *The General Theory of Employment, Interest and Money,* published in 1936, may have served to inspire the policies of the postwar world, but, paradoxically for a work that so caught the popular imagination, it was addressed not to the public, nor even to policymakers, but to Keynes's fellow economists. Keynes believed that policy had been led astray because it had been built on poor foundations, and his goal was to provide new foundations.

Keynes's theory was based on what he believed were fundamental insights about the world that were, he claimed, different from those that underlay the work of his contemporaries and predecessors—the economists he chose, with considerable injustice, to lump together under the label of "classical economists." His main insight was the idea that the level of economic activity was determined by what he called "effective demand" for goods and services. If people were to spend more, the result would be higher production and, paradoxically, higher incomes. The result was that rises in government spending or tax cuts (which increase private spending) would raise production and reduce unemployment, at least in circumstances such as the Great Depression when there was massive unused industrial capacity. But beneath this insight lay something deeper, which provided the reason why free markets might, on their own, be unable to generate full employment.

Keynes contended that we live in a world that is uncertain and have to make decisions without knowing what the full consequences of our actions will be. This is especially true of business investment—decisions to buy the buildings, machinery, and other capital goods that increase a nation's productive capacity—in which decisions have to be made about projects that may yield their returns over many years. Thus he wrote:

> The outstanding fact is the extreme precariousness of the basis of the knowledge on which our estimates of prospective yields have to be made. Our knowledge of the factors which will govern the yield of an investment some years hence is usually very slight and often negligible. If we speak frankly, we have to admit that the basis of knowledge for estimating the yield ten years hence of a railway, a copper mine, a textile factory, the goodwill of a patent medicine, an Atlantic liner, a building in the City of London amounts to little and sometimes to nothing; or even five years hence.[1]

Furthermore, this uncertainty means that financial markets cannot be trusted to coordinate saving and investment decisions, for the same uncertainty applies to the yields on many financial assets. The future return on equities is as unknowable as that on the capital assets they represent, which means that markets have to fall back on conventional valuations. Thus investors "are concerned not with what an investment is worth to a man who buys it 'for keeps,' but with what the market will value it at, under the influence of mass psychology, three months or a year hence." He went on: "The social object of skilled investment should be to defeat the dark forces of time and ignorance which envelop our future. The actual, private object of the most skilled investment today is 'to beat the gun,' as the Americans so well express it, to outwit the crowd, and to pass the bad, or depreciating, half-crown to the other fellow."[2] Keynes concluded that there was no reason to believe that the most profitable investment strategy would also be the most socially advantageous one. Enterprise had become "the bubble on a whirlpool of speculation."[3] The market, he believed, had become too liquid in the sense that it had become too easy to buy and sell investments. Investment needed, he suggested, a substantial tax on each sale of stock, which would make quick turnover of ownership less profitable and would rule out a large proportion of the transactions on Wall Street, restoring the balance between enterprise and speculation. It would be a step toward making investment contracts "permanent and indissoluble, like marriage."[4]

In passages like these, Keynes outlined a perspective on how capitalist economies operated that, in the aftermath of the recent financial crisis, has great intuitive appeal. However, economic theorizing involves more than having the right intuitions about how the economy works. Such beliefs, however well grounded in observations of financial markets, need to be translated into a system that can be analyzed so that we can find out whether what appear to be profound insights are indeed that, and not merely something incidental to the main problems that need to be tackled. In short, they need to be turned into a usable economic theory. Because the economy is so complex, it becomes necessary to abstract from many of the details that anchor the economy in our own experiences, picking out those features of the world that are believed to be important. This is where economics becomes hard for outsiders to understand, for economic theory explores how abstract agents interact in idealized markets. In order to make theories that are amenable to analysis using logical or mathematical argument and that can be tested against a wide range of evidence, economic theorists deal with worlds that are inevitably simplifications of the world we know around us.

In *The General Theory,* Keynes challenged the abstractions and simplifications that his predecessors had used in their attempts to make sense of the complexity of twentieth-century capitalism. They were, he argued, like "Euclidian geometers in a non-Euclidian world,"[5] trying to analyze an uncertain world using tools that were appropriate only for a world in which people could know the future with certainty. Yet because abstraction and idealization are an inevitable part of any economic theory he could not dispense with such methods altogether. He had to argue for a different set of abstractions—for a new set of conceptual tools with which to analyze, or model, the economy. These new tools gave Keynes the freedom to describe the economy in new ways; he was able to build narratives about unemployment and stagnation that were not possible with the old ones. The subsequent Keynesian revolution in economic theory came about when economists started using these concepts to create new models of how the economy worked. This was true even of economists who came to oppose Keynesian policies, such as Milton Friedman, the doyen of monetarism and free-market economics:

though they might not be Keynesians, in that they did not accept Keynes's policy recommendations, they used many of the tools and concepts Keynes had developed.

Because the decade after *The General Theory* was published was the time when economists were turning to the use of mathematics in a big way, the models that constituted the Keynesian revolution in economic theory were mathematical—systems of equations that described abstract economies and could be used to show how those economies would respond when, for example, the government increased its spending on goods and services, or cut the money supply. Whereas Keynes was constantly looking for ways to more effectively explain the economic maladies that he saw around him, even if it meant using looser, more open methods, the economists who followed Keynes became much more concerned with the internal consistency of their models, creating a completely different style of theorizing about the economy.

This new type of economic theory gives another reason why Keynes was seen differently by different generations of economists. Quite apart from the changes that led to different conceptions of economic policy, economists developed new ways to construct economic theory. Not only did they learn new mathematical tools, but they also changed their views on what abstractions it was appropriate to make. In the 1940s and 1950s economists were open to a range of ideas about human psychology—it was an age when what was termed "the human factor" was seen as lying at the center of most problems in social science. However, over the next two decades they turned increasingly to rational-choice theory.

Rational-choice theory is based on a very simple account of human motivation in that people are taken to be abstract agents who always choose the best out of all the possibilities that are available to them. In this view, the economist has no business questioning the preferences on which these choices are based, but merely assumes that they are consistent. The theory applies to everyone, whether the manager of a corporation or an individual worker or consumer. The rise of rational-choice theory in economics meant that Keynesian economic theory had to be reinterpreted, for Keynes had based his theories on his own observations about how people actually behaved, not on the assumption that all choices were rational. The result was that his theories, and those of the early Keynesians, because they were not based on models of rational choice, were taken to have no legitimate explanation of how individuals behaved. Theories that had been cutting-edge in the 1940s were by the 1970s considered too primitive to be taken seriously. But this meant that economists came to see *The General Theory* through the lens of rational-choice theory: arguments that could not be fitted into this framework were not seen as being legitimate economic theory, with the result that economists who read *The General Theory* began to see a different work from the one that had been seen, even by economists, in the 1940s.

Changing conventions about what constitutes a respectable economic theory would alone be enough to explain why it has become difficult for modern economists to see Keynes as he appeared a generation ago. This difficulty is exacerbated by the fact that Keynes was not a narrow, academic economist but was a person of many interests, whose work drew on sources that are foreign to the much more specialized academic discipline that exists today. The philosophical and moral background to his thinking that we will consider shortly gave him an understanding of the world that may have been unique among twentieth-century economists. It led him to an understanding of economics that is very different from the concept of the discipline as a "modeling science" that came to prevail after the Second World War. Thus, to understand Keynes as an economic theorist, let alone as the designer of economic policy, we need to explain how Keynes saw the world.

To some degree, what sets Keynes apart from many contemporary economists was his vision of economics as a tool for diagnosing the economy. Keynes saw himself as playing a role much like that of a physician examining a patient: economic theory was a diagnostic tool that could help him explain the maladies of a capitalist economy. It thus had to be serviceable and useful for examining the problems with which he was confronted. He was not committed to the eternal truth of his theories in the same way that many modern economists are committed to models based on rational choice. When the maladies changed, he was willing to change his theory and did not claim that there was one theory that was good for all time. To the contrary, to set up such a theory would be to establish an orthodoxy, something to which, as we shall see, he was passionately opposed.

Keynesian economics has come to be associated with the Great Depression and the problem of mass unemployment because this was the background to *The General Theory*. But to understand Keynes's work it is important to realize that his ideas changed because the problems he was analyzing changed. In the years between the First and Second World Wars, Britain suffered prolonged economic stagnation. Even as the United States boomed ("the roaring twenties"), from 1924 to 1939, unemployment in his native Britain fell below 10 percent in only one year (1927); and in the industrial north, where the coal, steel, shipbuilding, and textile industries were in dire straits, it was much higher. It was not till 1940, after Britain had mobilized its resources for war, that unemployment fell below this level. His three best-known books on monetary economics—*A Tract on Monetary Reform* (1923), *A Treatise on Money* (1930), and *The General Theory of Employment, Interest and Money* (1936)—can be seen as an ongoing effort to discover a means to explain why the British economy was performing so badly. The persistence of unemployment for such a prolonged period also explains why Keynes did not see laissez-faire as an adequate explanation of the ills that plagued the British economy. Something was broken, and he wanted to find a means to identify exactly what was wrong.

The main reason why economists have changed their theories is that they have been concerned to be "scientific": this is why they have sought to develop rigorous, general theories. In order to make their models completely rigorous, they have had to deal with very simple worlds, for otherwise the math would get impossibly complicated. In modern macroeconomics, simplicity has been achieved through the device of the "representative agent": not only are agents rational maximizers, but they are all exactly alike. This notion simplifies modeling enormously because it assumes that the economy as a whole behaves exactly like the individuals of which it is composed. Macroeconomic theory is thereby given highly mathematically rigorous microeconomic foundations. However, the price of this approach is that, if all agents are identical, there can never be coordination failures: it is impossible for the behavior of some individuals to be incompatible with the behavior of other individuals. For example, it is impossible for firms to make investment decisions that are incompatible with households' decisions about what to save, because these decisions are all taken by individuals who are identical.

This erasing of the differences between people is in dramatic contrast with the approach of Keynes, who traced many of society's problems to inconsistencies between the expectations and activities of different groups of people. Businessmen, investors, speculators, consumers, and government officials exhibited different behaviors that, even if they were rational for the individuals concerned, might interact to produce disastrous social consequences. In *The General Theory* this complexity comes out in several ways. Financial markets are driven by differences between investors' expectations, for otherwise speculative trades would be impossible. In order to explain these expectations, Keynes was led into an exploration of the social psychology of investment. Decisions about how much to save and how much to invest were the outcomes of different types of reasoning, with the result that there was no reason to assume that they would be consistent with full employment. And there could be no presumption that workers and their employers would see the future in the same way. This view of the world, in which people play different roles, which underpinned virtually everything Keynes wrote, would have made sense to almost all his predecessors and contemporaries—most especially to Adam Smith—and it was integral to his early writings on the effects of the First World War, but it has been abandoned in some of the most prominent parts of modern macroeconomics.

But it is impossible to wonder whether economists' commitment to the rational-choice and representative-agent models, which fit ill with much that Keynes believed about the world, may also have taken hold because, especially in the past three to four decades, there has been a bias toward developing theories that show how markets can produce better outcomes than the government can. Economists have produced theories that show how rational economic agents operating in free markets can do better than they could if government intervened and in which the result of government intervention will normally be to make things worse. Such economists have a vision of capitalism as inherently stable, in marked contrast to Keynes's vision of capitalism as being potentially unstable and needing to be carefully managed. To make their case against the theories and policies they were challenging, they attacked stereotypes of Keynes, who came to personify the least subtle versions of Keynesian economics that had emerged by the 1960s. For some he was the economist who undermined the idea that the state should balance its budget; for others he laid the foundations for the excessively elaborate forecasting models based on flawed conceptual foundations.

Keynes the Moral Philosopher

As if all this were not enough, there is yet another Keynes to consider. In 1936, when noneconomists read *The General Theory,* induced by Keynes's fame and the very low price at which it was sold, many of them were baffled by the economic theory, seeing it as abstruse mathematics. What they could understand, aside from the fact that Keynes was attacking an orthodoxy called "classical economics," was not his recommendations about fiscal policy, for the book offered few of these; it was his concluding chapter on the social philosophy toward which his ideas might lead. In laying out a vision of how society ought to be organized, Keynes was going beyond the remit of the economist, venturing into the realm of the philosopher. And not for the first time, for one of the themes running through his work from the *Economic Consequences of the Peace* onward had been a moral critique of capitalism. He approached economics as a moral philosopher.

Because so much of modern macroeconomics draws on concepts and theories he proposed, albeit combined with assumptions that he did not make and in a theoretical framework that was not his, it is natural for contemporary economists to conclude that Keynes was doing the same thing that they are doing when they create models of the economy. It only makes matters worse that Keynes was educated as a mathematician and often expressed himself using mathematical language, and the symbols of mathematical formalism, for all of this makes Keynes look and sound like a modern economist. But although Keynes was responsible for developing and propagating some of the concepts on which modern economics rests, he imagined people using economic theories in ways that were very different from the ways in which economists have subsequently come to use models. To understand this, we need to examine his engagements with philosophy.

In his early career, Keynes was an active participant in the world of Cambridge philosophy—the world of G. E. Moore, Bertrand Russell, and, later, Ludwig Wittgenstein and Frank Ramsey. The dissertation he submitted in 1908 to obtain his fellowship at King's College Cambridge dealt with the philosophy of probability and was later developed into a major philosophical work, *A Treatise on Probability* (1921). Much of this work drew from his involvement as a member of the Apostles, a secret Cambridge club that met on Saturday evenings during term and that Keynes joined as an undergraduate student. The most prominent Cambridge philosophers in the generation before Keynes were members, and the youngest of these, G. E. Moore, was a don at Cambridge when Keynes arrived. Moore often attended the Saturday evening meetings at which the undergraduates discussed each other's papers, and his influence shaped Keynes's life.

Keynes's work in philosophy drew heavily from questions that Moore raised in his own work about how to make ethical decisions when one does not know with certainty what the outcome of one's actions will be. Thus, Keynes was concerned both with ethics and with questions about the nature of probable, uncertain knowledge. On the one hand, this work gave Keynes a deep background in ethics; on the other hand, it caused him to reject the utilitarian philosophy that underpins much of contemporary economics.

Hence the ground for yet more confusion and misunderstanding as regards the nature of Keynes's theoretical work. The elegant models developed by economic theorists in the second half of the twentieth century depended on common assumptions about human behavior that preclude the kind of ethical distinctions that were central to Keynes's own self-understanding. Although economists in the second half of the twentieth century were correct that Keynes was an economic theorist, they could not easily recognize either the loose way in which Keynes used those models for diagnostic purposes, or the different ethical approach he took to evaluating economic problems such as long-term unemployment.

Other Apostles in Keynes's generation came to hold many of the same values and concerns as he did. In order to better understand the way that he weighed the social and political costs of unemployment, for instance, one could look to the way that other Apostles of his generation wrote about its costs. One could look to E. M. Forster's novel *Howards End* to grasp some sense of the human degradation that Keynes believed was caused by unemployment. Likewise, one could consider the work of the political philosopher Leonard Woolf to grasp the potential Keynes saw for the political instability that unemployment might cause.

Without this broader perspective on Keynes's work, we too easily lose sight of what he thought was important about his diagnoses of capitalism and hence fail to understand him fully as an economic theorist.

The Historical Keynes

As with any historical figure whose ideas have contemporary political currency, the Keynes of the popular imagination is to a large extent a caricature. The same can be said of the popular conception of his ideas on economic policy—what we infelicitously call Keynesianism. During his lifetime, Keynes was the frequent subject of political cartoonists who loved to capture his thick lips and large eyes in their drawings. In a similar fashion, Keynes's work in economic theory and economic policy is easily subject to caricature. Keynes took on some of the biggest shibboleths of his generation, and he had the audacity to offer theoretical explanations of market capitalism that did not demonstrate that it always and on all occasions would provide the best possible outcome. Anyone whose ideas are large and bold enough to challenge laissez-faire economics would easily be subject to exaggeration and caricature.

But beyond the fact that his bold ideas are easy to exaggerate, there are other aspects of Keynes's work that make it easy to misunderstand. Ironically, many of the aspects of his work that make it so adaptable to both good times and bad are also the aspects of it that make it easy to misunderstand. One of our purposes in this book is to show why Keynes's ideas are applicable to such a variety of circumstances: to show why, for example, his best-known work, *The General Theory,* has been useful to people who were trying to make very different kinds of policy recommendations on the basis of different visions of the fundamental nature of a capitalist economy.

Our goal is not to argue that one aspect of Keynes should be placed on a pedestal and the others debunked. Instead, we seek to explain why Keynes can legitimately be seen to have laid the groundwork for seeing the economy in several different lights. We will try to demonstrate why some of the worst stereotypes are neither reasonable representations of his work, nor good ways to understand the *potential* in his work. In the process, we will reveal a subtle mind that rejected many aspects of capitalism, yet felt that it was the ultimately the best economic system available.

2

THE RISE AND FALL OF KEYNESIAN ECONOMICS

The Myth of the Keynesian Revolution

For good or for ill, Keynesian economics is often argued to have transformed economic policymaking in the industrial democracies after the Great Depression. At one time, it was common to refer to Keynes as "the man who saved capitalism" during the Great Depression. The gist of this story is that in *The General Theory of Employment, Interest and Money,* published in 1936, Keynes provided a revolutionary analysis of how capitalist economies worked, completely rejecting over a hundred years of "classical" economic theorizing by showing how fiscal policy could be used to maintain a high level of employment; and that politicians embraced these ideas, thereby pulling their countries back from the brink of collapse. Boldly venturing into the use of deficit spending, politicians were thought to have drawn their main inspiration from Keynes's writings, without which the Great Depression might have persisted far longer.

But like many potted histories, this one bears little or no resemblance to reality. Take first the relationship of Keynes's theory to that of his predecessors and contemporaries. Keynes himself fostered the idea that he was fomenting a revolution in economic theory, overthrowing a dominant orthodoxy. A year before the book appeared, he wrote, in a much-quoted remark to the playwright and socialist intellectual, George Bernard Shaw, "I believe myself to be writing a book on economic theory which will largely revolutionize—not, I suppose, at once, but in the course of the next ten years—the way the world thinks about economic problems."[1] In *The General Theory* he took up this idea, writing of his own "struggle of escape from habitual modes of thought and expression" and framing his own ideas as a theory that was more general than the classical theory, as we mentioned earlier, likening his predecessors to "Euclidian geometers in a non-Euclidian world." He drew an implicit parallel between what he was doing in economics and what Einstein had done in physics. This theme of a revolution in economics was taken up by many of his followers and eventually became a dogma, accepted by supporters and enemies alike.

There was, without any doubt whatsoever, what David Laidler has called "a major re-arrangement of [economic] ideas in the late 1930s," though he went on to claim that "an element of myth-making is involved whenever the phrase 'Keynesian revolution' is deployed."[2] His reasoning was that the rearrangement of ideas that we describe this way was neither revolutionary in the usual sense of the word nor by any means uniquely Keynesian in origin. In other words, the changes that we refer to as the Keynesian revolution did not amount to a complete overthrow of previous ideas and were not brought about by Keynes alone.

The justification for this view is that *The General Theory* built on two decades of remarkably creative theorizing about problems of the business cycle and unemployment, by Keynes himself as well as by economists he lambasted as "classical." Since the turn of the twentieth century, economists had been analyzing the causes of the business cycle, a term that was popularized in the 1920s as "Business Cycle Institutes" appeared in country after country, of which Wesley Mitchell's National Bureau of Economic Research, established in 1919 in the United States, was the most notable example. These sought to develop and analyze statistics on business fluctuations—to create accurate statistical pictures of what actually happened over the cycle—and thereby to better understand them.

Economists might (as did Keynes himself) use the traditional quantity theory of money (which postulated a long-run relationship between the money supply—the stock of currency and bank deposits—and the price level) as their analytical framework; but this was sufficiently flexible to allow economists to pursue many different ideas about what caused the cycle and fluctuations in the rate of unemployment. Drawing on theories of the business cycle that stretched back into the nineteenth century, Keynes and his Cambridge colleague Arthur Cecil Pigou emphasized the role of businessmen's expectations in causing the cycle; Ralph Hawtrey, a Cambridge-trained economist who spent much of the interwar period as the British Treasury's only specialist, in-house economist focused on the role of the money markets in exacerbating cyclical fluctuations. In continental Europe, Swedish economists developed monetary theories that amounted almost to an abandoning of the quantity theory, replacing it with theories much closer to the theories to which Keynes turned in the 1930s. And Austrians, including Ludwig von Mises and Friedrich Hayek (who in the 1970s was to be a strong influence on Margaret Thatcher and Ronald Reagan), argued that the cycle was caused by overexpansionary monetary policy leading to unsustainable booms that would inevitably collapse into recession. In the United States, the need of the newly established Federal Reserve System to develop operating rules led to a proliferation of work on monetary policy and the cycle. Even at the University of Chicago, now seen as the home of free-market, anti-Keynesian theory, Henry Simons made the case for active government intervention to stabilize the economy.

Though Keynes did propose a new theory, he built it out of concepts that were developed during the 1920s and 1930s. The distinction between saving (deciding not to spend all of one's income on consumption goods) and investment (deciding to spend money on buying capital goods, such as new buildings, machinery, or transport facilities, that would raise output in the future) that was central to Keynes's theory had been developed in the 1920s by Keynes and his colleague Dennis Robertson (who later objected to Keynes's claim to be mounting a revolution). The theory of the marginal efficiency of capital—Keynes's theory of investment—was heavily influenced by the work of the American quantity theorist Irving Fisher. Much of Keynes's theory about why people held money drew on earlier work at Cambridge and elsewhere. Keynes claimed that what distinguished his own theory from "classical" theory was recognition of the idea of effective demand—the demand for goods and services as a whole—but not only the idea but also the phrase had been used by Hawtrey before the First World War. Virtually all the concepts Keynes used had been developed earlier, and some had become very widely accepted before *The General Theory* appeared. Furthermore, though Keynes was innovative, his theorizing could legitimately be criticized by the prominent Swedish economist Bertil Ohlin (who was leader of the Liberal Party for two decades after the Second World War and won the Nobel Memorial Prize for his work on international economics) as being very conservative, spurning the explicit dynamic analysis being undertaken in Sweden, and which Keynes himself had explored in 1930. Keynes was important not because he overthrew everything that went before, but because his *General Theory* became the channel through which a wealth of creative thinking about the business cycle was transmitted into postwar economics.

This is not to say that economists did not hold any of the views Keynes criticized them for holding. Some did. The conservative views of Mises and Hayek, who argued that government policy exacerbated rather than smoothed the business cycle, have already been mentioned. In Britain, they were taken up by Lionel Robbins, and in the United States, similar views were held by Alvin Hansen (later to become a convert to Keynes). Hawtrey, one of Keynes's contemporaries at Cambridge, was one of the main proponents of the so-called Treasury View—the doctrine that if the government borrowed money to fund public-works programs (to build roads, schools, and other investment projects), those funds would be taken away from private investment, with the result that there would be no net effect on employment. Other economists feared that expansionary policy would cause inflation, and so suggested that when countries were faced with mounting budget deficits as the world economy collapsed into depression, the remedy should be to cut government spending in order to get these deficits under control. Without balanced budgets there would be inflationary pressure and investors would not have confidence in the value of money.

But this does not mean that there was a monolithic orthodoxy, either within economic theory or about economic policy: there was a wide range of views. This is well illustrated by the debates that took place in the 1920s over how the newly established Federal Reserve System should conduct monetary policy. The range of views extended from those who took a hard line on inflation, arguing that the Fed should pursue a tight monetary policy, to those who claimed that the Fed should allow the money supply to meet the needs of business, on the grounds that if business did not have productive uses for borrowed funds, no borrowing would take place. There were advocates of monetary rules (such as Irving Fisher, who proposed a series of rules that he believed would stabilize the value of the dollar) and advocates of discretion (believing that the Fed should learn how to actively use monetary policy to manage the economy).

What happened was that, for reasons that need to be explored, Keynes's *General Theory* ended up being the vehicle through which these theoretical ideas, worked out in the 1920s and early 1930s, entered modern economics. *The General Theory* acted as a filter, some ideas making it through and others getting lost. The result was that, when they looked back, later generations of economists saw Keynes looming so large not because he had created the subject from scratch but because they saw the past through the lens of Keynesian economics.

The potted history with which we started this chapter is also wrong on the policy front. There were, indeed, nations that experimented with deficit spending in the 1920s and 1930s, but the awkward fact is that in none of them had the policymakers got the idea of using deficits from reading Keynes's great book. Not in Sweden; not in Germany; not in Japan; not in France; not in the United States; and certainly not in Britain, where there was never any serious experiment during the interwar years with government budget deficits.

In Sweden, the emergence of government budget deficits came in the 1930s through the creation of a political coalition between rural farmers and urban laborers, two groups who had traditionally been at odds in Swedish politics. Before the Great Depression, the farmers wanted high food prices and low prices for manufactured goods; industrial workers wanted high prices for manufactured goods and low prices for food. The two groups were able to find common ground through the political entrepreneurship of the political parties that had traditionally represented them, resulting in a program that would create jobs in the cities and subsidize farm income in the countryside.

Keynes had been the main opponent of the French attempt to extract high reparations from Germany at the Versailles peace conference, and his stance produced resentment toward him. It is therefore not surprising that *The General Theory* was not translated into French until 1942, and was not available in France in English until after the Second World War. Germans were more receptive to Keynes's views, but in Germany the use of deficits was a pragmatic political alternative during the Weimar Republic endorsed by both business and labor. Faced with an explosion of inflation after the First World War, all classes in German society suffered from economic hardship. Only by offering tax cuts to businesses and increasing expenditure on social programs supported by labor groups was it possible to create a ruling coalition in the deteriorating political environment of hyperinflation. The deficits run during the Weimar Republic have been described as the "social cement" that held the nation together,[3] whereas under the Nazis government spending was driven by rearmament, not by its effects on aggregate demand. The use of deficit spending in the 1930s in Japan was the direct result of the intervention of the military in the government's fiscal policy. The leaders of the military demanded a robust rearmament program and intervened to get it even though the finance minister argued that there were insufficient tax revenues for what he was being asked to do.

Because Franklin Roosevelt's New Deal is so often associated, in the popular mind, with Keynesian ideas, it is worth looking especially carefully at what happened in America. In his first two campaigns for the presidency, Roosevelt ran on a strong platform of balancing the budget. In fact in the 1932 campaign he depicted Herbert Hoover as a dangerous profligate because the federal budget was in deficit. Hoover, of course, had never intended to run a deficit, but rather had been the victim of rapidly falling tax revenues when the economy had slumped after the stock market crash in 1929. Roosevelt's first New Deal, his economic policy during his first term in office, consisted, on the one hand, of plans to raise industrial output by diminishing the monopoly power of big business and, on the other hand, a plan to buy gold to raise its price. The National Recovery Administration, in operation from 1932 to 1935, was based not on providing a fiscal stimulus, but rather on the belief that markets had to be stabilized, using price controls where necessary, with prices being set to balance the interests of various groups in American society. Roosevelt did end up presiding over deficits in the federal budget in his first term, but, like Hoover's deficits, these were unintentional, and he blamed them on the emergency relief expenditures that he had undertaken after his election when the severity of the Depression had become fully clear to him. One of the prime examples that Roosevelt used in making his argument about the unintentional deficits was the Civilian Conservation Corps, a highly popular program that had been funded for a fixed period with a strictly limited budget. He redoubled his promise to balance the budget in his 1936 campaign, arguing that this was now possible since relief was no longer so urgently needed.

Not long after his second inauguration in 1937, however, Roosevelt faced an unfolding crisis when his advisers realized that the economy was headed into a second slump. When he first intentionally used a government budget deficit to stimulate the American economy, in his 1938 budget, he drew on the ideas of several young researchers in his own government, none of whom had got the idea from reading Keynes. Using federal budget data, researchers discovered that the slump had been preceded by a double tightening on the fiscal side: the last bonus payment for veterans of the First World War had been made in 1936, and the first tax collections for Social Security had been levied in 1937, resulting in a fiscal contraction of over 5 percent. Harry Hopkins, who served as Roosevelt's secretary of commerce at the time, used these figures to convince Roosevelt that the budgetary surplus created by these two actions was responsible for the slump in general economic activity. Thus, no one who had advocated the initial planned deficit for the 1938 budget was drawing from Keynes's work in making the recommendation. By 1940, Keynes's ideas had begun to show up in Roosevelt's administration, but they were used then as a technical apparatus to explain policies that had already been decided on for other reasons.

Even in Britain, where Keynes himself moved in and out of the corridors of power, and was appointed as a special consultant to the Treasury during the Second World War, the government never adopted a policy of fiscal stimulus during his lifetime. The first clear influence of Keynes's ideas in British policymaking had nothing to do with stimulating the economy but had to do with controlling inflation. Keynes's ideas were first used explicitly in 1941, when the urgent need for higher military spending meant that demand for resources far exceeded supply. Keynesian ideas were used as a framework for working out how much civilian consumption needed to be reduced and how higher taxes, compulsory savings, and other measures could be used to achieve this reduction without causing prices to rise. The first British application of the ideas Keynes had developed in *The General Theory* concerned the problem of "How to Pay for the War," to quote the title of a pamphlet he wrote in 1940. This work showed clearly how he could adapt his theory when the problems he was facing changed.

Perhaps the only country where we know unequivocally that Keynes's ideas influenced the government was Canada, where several young economists who studied under Keynes in the 1930s at Cambridge returned home and entered the civil service in time to influence the government to use fiscal policy to attempt to help the country out of the Depression. Canada, however, stands out as an exception to the norm, which is of budget deficits arising for reasons unconnected with Keynes.

What actually happened in policymaking, as in economic theory, was more complicated and, in a sense, more profound than the common view of what the Keynesian revolution entailed. There was a deep-seated change in attitudes toward government policy that was the result of many political and social factors, to which Keynes's name came to be attached. Of course, many of his ideas could be used to support this changed view of policymaking, but he bore little responsibility for the details of the policy that emerged. His name came to be attached to these policies because, after his death, in what came to be called "The Age of Keynes," his theories provided a common language in which to talk about the fiscal policy experiments that were being undertaken in many countries.

The Age of Keynes

If *The General Theory* did not cause a complete break with previous theories about how capitalist economies work and if his work was not the cause of the transformation in the way governments approached economic policy, how is it that the period from the Second World War to the oil shocks of the 1970s came to be known as the age of Keynes? To answer this question, it is easiest to start with economic policy, turning afterward to economic theory.

After the Second World War, even though demand-management policies had been introduced before the war for reasons that had little to do with Keynes, Keynes and Keynesianism became closely identified with macroeconomic planning and especially with the use of government budget deficits to control the level of economic activity. If the economy entered a recession, either government spending needed to be increased or taxes cut so as to stimulate demand, maintaining full employment; conversely, if the economy became overheated, with over-full employment creating inflationary pressure, the deficit needed to be reduced, thereby restoring balance between aggregate demand and what the economy was capable of producing. To see why this came about, we need to understand, first, why this new approach to economic policy emerged and, second, why Keynes's name came to be attached to it.

The underlying reason for the emergence of the view that government should manage the level of demand in this way was the widespread postwar belief that the immense spending on the Second World War had been responsible for ending the Great Depression. The industrialized economies had never fully recovered before the war, but during the war unemployment was virtually eliminated. As a result there emerged a widely held belief that government expenditure was the reason for what were for the United States the best of (economic) times in almost two decades (other countries such as Britain might be suffering from austerity, but this was for other reasons). Thus, there was a political demand for more demand management following the war.

For policymakers, the rise of social democratic ideals and the welfare state following the war also led to the popularity of demand management. The deprivations of the Depression had created a strong political demand for greater social justice, as had the sacrifices of working men and women during the war itself. Many of the experiments with deficit spending before the war (for example, in Sweden, France, and Germany) had involved redistributive policies, and William Beveridge's work on the welfare state in Britain during the war was widely known across the industrialized democracies by 1945. Beveridge had made an explicit argument in his work for the necessity of maintaining full employment as an important element of the welfare state. His argument made sense for several reasons: not only did it seem equitable to maintain high employment, but high employment would also mean that there would be fewer people in need of social security payments and that tax revenues would be higher. Thus, the use of demand-management policies to maintain full employment seemed like a logical strategy for politicians in the postwar world: indeed, the maintenance of full employment may have been a necessary condition for welfare states to be affordable.

Demand management also gained credence as a necessary part of effective economic policy because of the Cold War. One of the ways to demonstrate the superiority of capitalism was to make sure that it always provided full employment, something the

Soviet Union could claim to ensure through its system of central planning, and demand management still looked like the best means to avoid the failures that had characterized the Great Depression. In this sense, demand management was seen as a part of the technological apparatus that the West was adding to its arsenal of ideas.

A further reason for the changed attitude to policy has to do with the complex relationship that was then emerging between professional economists and politicians. By the time Keynes published his *General Theory* in 1936, there had begun to emerge a widespread demand for expert economic advice on how to best manage the economy. While economists had been trying to construct theories about the economy for at least two centuries by 1936, these had never been understood to have the power to explain the economy with the precision that economists were beginning to strive for when they started to use mathematics and statistics more widely in the 1920s and 1930s. And while there had been many downturns in economic activity during the industrialization of the Western economies, the Great Depression was so prolonged and so severe that politicians found it impossible not to look for the means to improve the economy's performance.

The Second World War propelled a stage further this move toward seeing economics as a form of engineering that could be used to design a more efficient economic system than the laissez-faire capitalism that had failed the world in the 1930s. Mobilizing resources for war had required planning. Roosevelt's "Victory Program" required a massive increase in military spending, and economists Simon Kuznets and Robert Nathan used the newly developed national accounts to help in organizing and rationalizing the planning process: the share of U.S. national income accounted for by military procurement rose from 4 to 48 percent (it is easily forgotten how limited America's military capacity was in 1940). This involvement in planning the U.S. economy, like the activities of other economists working in government service, was part of a much broader involvement of social scientists in the war effort: anthropologists and geographers provided intelligence on unknown parts of the world; political scientists and sociologists analyzed enemy countries, the better to design propaganda; and psychologists were needed everywhere, from screening recruits in order to avoid psychological casualties (a task in which they demonstrably failed) to understanding how the enemy behaved. Moreover, economists were not just involved in economic planning: they were employed alongside natural scientists (and other social scientists) in the Office of Strategic Services (the forerunner of the Central Intelligence Agency). Economists not only estimated German and Japanese economic capacity and worked out how best to allocate scarce shipping capacity, but worked alongside mathematicians, statisticians, and scientists as members of a cadre of general problem-solvers, who helped solve technical military problems such as how to design aircraft gunsights and how to prevent shells targeted at the enemy from accidentally falling on their own troops. Thus, Paul Samuelson could later claim that the Second World War, generally known as the physicists' war on account of the technical advances from radar and the jet engine to the atomic bomb that contributed to the Allied victory, was equally "the economists' war."[4] Economics emerged from the Second World War with its reputation greatly enhanced.

Thus, the postwar world represented a unique moment in which economists believed they were at last attaining the ability to analyze the economy and to offer scientific advice on how various ends could be achieved, and politicians were looking for models that could help them design effective policies. Keynesian economics had the enormous merit of representing what was seen, using a phrase popularized by Harold Macmillan, British prime minister from 1956 to 1963, as "the middle way" between socialist central planning and the free-market capitalism that had failed so calamitously in the Great Depression. But it was more than that: it opened up a way of analyzing the economy that meshed with contemporary views of science.

If economics was to become more scientific, it needed to develop theories with more predictive power—that could make economics more like engineering. In order to achieve this, even if the general public and even some policymakers were only dimly aware of what was happening, they developed an increasingly elaborate apparatus of mathematical economic theory: formal sets of propositions about how market economies actually behaved that could be analyzed rigorously using increasingly advanced mathematical tools. Policy propositions purportedly rested not on political philosophies or even theories based on purely verbal reasoning, but on "models"—mathematical structures that could be used to predict what would happen in the event of certain shocks hitting the economy or of policy levers being pulled forward or backward.

There were several reasons why it made sense to use Keynes's *General Theory* as the starting point for such modeling. Keynes's theory might be too simple for some tastes (the great Harvard economist and onetime Austrian finance minister, J. A. Schumpeter, a prominent student of the business cycle, dismissed the three key components of the *General Theory* as "the three great simplifiers"),[5] and his policy preferences might not appeal to others, but his theory provided a new way to think about the economic system as a whole. Milton Friedman, who in the 1970s became the most successful opponent of Keynesian policies, said that Keynes caused economists, even those who did not accept his views on policy, to see the world through new lenses and that he had provided new tools that they could use.

One of the main reasons why Keynes's ideas became central to postwar economics was that a major change occurred in the way economists analyzed the economy. Though others had constructed mathematical models of the business cycle (notably Ragnar Frisch and Jan Tinbergen, who later became the first recipients of the Nobel Memorial Prize in Economics for their work), as soon as it was published, Keynes's *General Theory* provided, as did the work of no other economist, the theoretical framework within which mathematical modeling of the economy as a whole took place. Modern economists may complain about Keynes's lack of rigor (if only he had used more mathematics, they say, the book would have been so much clearer), but it is not often remembered that many of *The General Theory*'s reviewers in 1936 and 1937 had complained about the advanced mathematical treatment in the book. It was the new generation of mathematically trained economists to whom the book most appealed. Thus James Tobin wrote, thirty years later, of the immense appeal of Keynes's ideas to a young, quantitatively inclined economist.

However, although *The General Theory* contained the building blocks for a simple model of the economy as a whole, and although Keynes was a proficient mathematician and adopted a mathematical way of reasoning, for reasons we will discuss later he did not work with the simplified mathematical representations of the economy that economists increasingly called "models." He left that task to others. The result was that, almost immediately after *The General Theory* appeared, economists started to translate his ideas into algebra—into simple models that could be manipulated to produce "Keynesian" or "classical" results. The model that caught on was proposed by the British economist John Hicks in 1937, and was later renamed by Alvin Hansen, who was instrumental in bringing Keynesian ideas into American academia both through his seminar at Harvard and through his highly influential book, *A Guide to Keynes* (1953). It was a model that any student, once he or she had learned how to manipulate the curves correctly, could use to work out the effect of changing government spending or monetary policy. For many economists in the 1950s, the so-called IS-LM model, named after the labels attached to the two curves, *was* Keynesian economics.

Though students might be content with the IS-LM model, professional economists required more. One of the advantages of the model was that it could be complicated with additional equations that reflected the complexity of the economy. Theorists could develop more elaborate theories of saving and investment, and the models could take account of an increased range of phenomena. Yet, though these more complicated models might go beyond anything contemplated by Keynes, they were recognizably Keynesian in that their core consisted of ideas taken directly from *The General Theory*. Keynes thus dominated macroeconomic theory as much as he dominated policy in the 1950s and for much of the 1960s. Robert Barro, one of the free-market economists who transformed the discipline in the 1970s, has pointed out that when he turned to macroeconomics around 1970, Keynesian economics "seemed to be the only game in town."[6]

But theoretical models are of no use unless they can be related to what is going on in the economy. During the Second

World War, Keynes was closely involved with those who were creating the national accounts that defined the way gross national product was calculated, with the result that, by the end of the war, these accounts were organized into categories that exactly fit his model of aggregate demand. Whether Keynes drew more from the early pioneers of national income accounting, or vice versa, is not important; what matters is that just at the moment that statistical information became available on a scale of which earlier generations of economists could only dream, Keynes's model provided the natural framework for analyzing this information. Economists' empirical models—and this included the very large models used by governments to generate detailed forecasts of the effects of changes in policy—were thus constructed on Keynesian foundations.

Keynesian ideas remained important for as long as they did because for nearly three decades after the war, economists around the world were working in political and social milieus in which demand management had been used before the war and was now in vogue. Although the rise of demand management had been a matter of political invention in some countries and of collaboration with academic economists in others, Keynes's basic theoretical framework for describing demand management now became a common language for economists in a wide range of countries. Just as demand management had been introduced in the United States without any reference to Keynes's work, but later came to be explained within a Keynesian theoretical model, demand management also came to be explained in Keynesian terms in many other countries. In this sense, Keynes's work provided a universal outlook and a convenient way to talk about a common transnational phenomenon using one name: the Keynesian revolution. It did not hurt that the revolution was named after someone with international prestige and easy name recognition. It did not hurt either that, whether or not Keynesian policies were the reason for this success, the period was one of great prosperity: Germans saw an "economic miracle"; the French spoke of "les trentes glorieuses"; Britain, in the words of Prime Minister Harold Macmillan, "had never had it so good"; and the United States entered an "age of affluence."

The Demise of Keynesianism

Just as the Keynesian revolution and the age of Keynes have to be explained in relation to the political and social milieus in which they were located, so too does the end of the Keynesian era, when Keynesianism was displaced first by "monetarism" and after that by free-market economics. The revolution in economic policy defined by the use of demand management reached its apex in the 1960s. In the United States, President John F. Kennedy brought several of the leading Keynesian economists into his government as advisers and undertook the first explicit use of Keynesian ideas in the United States to run government fiscal policy. This move helped produce what at the time was the longest sustained peacetime economic growth in American history (1961–1968). Explicitly Keynesian ideas were also employed for the first time since the Second World War in West Germany and Japan during the 1960s, and their use in these two emerging economic powerhouses added to the sense of a revolution that had triumphed. The largest and strongest economies were now under Keynesian management, and those countries were prospering. The triumph of Keynesian ideas is often signified by the assertion "We are all Keynesians now," which was first attributed to Milton Friedman in December 1965 and which was later widely attributed to Richard Nixon in 1971 when he took the United States off the gold standard. But as is so often the case, this triumphal moment foreshadowed demise; Keynes and his ideas would soon be seen by many people as outdated, and by others as plain wrong. Two of the most forthright academic critics of Keynesianism whose ideas were becoming very influential by the end of the 1970s, Robert Lucas and Thomas Sargent, went so far as to claim that it was a simple matter of fact that Keynesian doctrines were fundamentally flawed and that "the task now facing contemporary students of the business cycle is to sort through the wreckage, determining which features of that remarkable intellectual event called the Keynesian Revolution can be salvaged and put to good use and which others must be discarded."[7] Of course, this was a highly polemical statement, written at a time when many economists were still defending Keynesian theories, but it illustrates the dramatic change that had taken place since the 1960s, when it would have been hard to conceive of any leading economist's making such a statement.

The proximate cause of the demise of the Keynesian influence that Richard Nixon so confidently trumpeted in 1971 was the stagflation that emerged later in the 1970s. Keynesian ideas had always been understood to be able to handle either inflation or unemployment. If the economy slowed and unemployment was rising, then a stimulus was in line. If the economy was overheating and inflation was rising, then policy should be tightened to dampen the economy. The problem in the 1970s was that there was no obvious way to use the Keynesian tools to address the appearance of inflation and unemployment simultaneously. The situation was even worse than this, however, for Keynesian ideas were not only seen as ineffective against the prevailing economic malaise; they were also being blamed for the malaise.

Keynesian policies were not to blame for what was happening in the 1970s. Neither was it true that Keynesian economists had failed to predict what would happen. The initial spur to inflation was President Lyndon Johnson's escalation of the Vietnam War while simultaneously trying to maintain a high level of expenditure on his War on Poverty. This combination of policies did not fully reflect the advice of his Keynesian advisers, who understood very well that it was possible to overstimulate the economy and ignite inflation. They had argued that, if the war was to be escalated, taxes needed to be raised, for they could see the potential inflationary consequences of not doing so. The escalation of the war without raising taxes produced a worldwide rise in commodity prices that culminated, soon after the Arab-Israeli October War in 1973, in two oil embargoes and a quadrupling of the price of oil. This transferred purchasing power to oil exporters, many of whom were in the Middle East, and who were unable or unwilling to increase their spending immediately. On the other hand, oil importers were forced, for financial reasons, to cut their spending straight away, the result being a collapse in world demand. At the same time, however, the oil price rise immediately pushed up inflation and caused many capital goods, unprofitable at high energy prices, to become obsolete. The result was stagflation—a sudden rise in both unemployment and the inflation rate.

Nonetheless, the critics of demand management saw an open opportunity and attacked Keynesianism not only as being ineffective against stagflation but as being responsible for the problem. Playing off this perception, a group of economists who were well funded by their conservative backers were quick to sharpen their attack against both Keynes and his ideas. The person who benefited most from this anti-Keynesian moment was Milton Friedman. Friedman was a brilliant empirical economist, originally trained as a statistician, with exceptional communication skills. In his 1967 presidential address to the American Economic Association, Friedman had made an eloquent appeal for a set of anti-Keynesian ideas called monetarism. Friedman had worked on these ideas for decades, but their appearance in his presidential address was widely noted, if only because they seemed so against the grain of the times. When Keynesianism came under attack in the 1970s, however, Friedman's ideas were the obvious alternative to which people could turn. The power of Friedman's ideas is perhaps best illustrated by the fact that Margaret Thatcher embraced them and used them in her campaign platform in 1979. Likewise, when Paul Volcker took over at the Federal Reserve in 1979, he explicitly embraced the policy recommendations that follow from Friedman's monetarist arguments.

Ironically, the broad range of Friedman's ideas held the seeds of their own demise. In addition to his strong advocacy of monetarism, a creed that recommended tight control of the money supply as the only effective macroeconomic policy, Friedman was a strong proponent of deregulating individual markets. Both Thatcher and Volcker instituted deregulation of financial markets as a part of their embrace of Friedman's ideas. For better or for worse, that financial market deregulation led to a destabilization of the financial relationships that undergirded the efficacy of Friedman's arguments in favor of tightly controlling the money supply. Because of changes in financial markets, both Thatcher and Volcker quickly found it necessary to abandon Friedman's strict edicts about how to conduct monetary policy. Holding the growth of the money supply to a low and steady rate of increase could not deliver the goods that Friedman had promised. In both Britain and the United States, the money supply was allowed to grow far beyond the targets that monetarists argued for during the mid-1980s; but the inflation that Friedman had predicted did not materialize.

But as Thatcher and Volcker abandoned Friedman's ideas, other brilliant young advocates of laissez-faire stepped forward to offer new models that purported to show that government intervention in the economy could only cause problems. Using complex statistical and mathematical tools that had been in the making for many years, these theorists offered simple and elegant theoretical models that showed that efforts by the government to improve economic performance would normally have the opposite effect. Some part of their revolution was undoubtedly predicated on their desire to build more technically sophisticated models that more accurately represented how the economy worked, but their results always pointed in one direction: the need to limit government economic policy. Through assuming "rational expectations" (loosely, that expectations of inflation are on average correct), a "representative agent" (that everyone in the economy is the same and all are perfect maximizers), and "continuous market clearing" (that supply and demand are equal in all markets, even the labor market, all the time), the advocates of laissez-faire offered new, theoretically sophisticated, cutting-edge models that came to be described by names such as the "New Classical Macroeconomics" and "Real Business Cycle Theory." By the 1990s, the work of these laissez-faire theorists dominated the profession to the extent that it was no longer thought necessary to speak of Keynes in discussions of economic policy. Both his ideas and the style of his theorizing had been so effectively eclipsed that he was not even the subject of serious discussion in economic policy.

The rise to prominence of the new proponents of laissez-faire at the end of the last century was perhaps not surprising. In the two decades following the stagflation of the 1970s, the industrial democracies had returned to robust health. In fact, they had become the *post*-industrial democracies. The immense wave of new investment spurred by the revolution in microchip technology and the advent of the Internet had spurred economic growth. In addition, most of the First World democracies had begun to pursue some form of more limited economic policymaking during the 1990s (such as balanced-budget rules and inflation targeting). The combination of a limited horizon for economic policymakers and strong private-sector growth seemed to bear out the basic argument of the new advocates of laissez-faire.

Rediscovering the Hidden Keynes

There *was* an age of Keynes. Keynes's *General Theory* pervaded economic theory and macroeconomic policymaking in the period from 1945 to the early 1970s. However, the reasons for this dominance lie deeper than conventional accounts of the Keynesian revolution suggest. It was an age of Keynes because changes in society and in intellectual life brought about profound changes in economics. Keynes's *General Theory* appeared at just the right time to be taken up and to shape these developments.

But though this was an age of Keynes, the way the transformation happened meant that the historical Keynes became obscured. It was assumed that the Keynesianism of the 1950s and 1960s was an accurate representation of Keynes's own views.

The result was that when there was a reaction against Keynesianism—on ideological grounds as much as because Keynesianism had failed—Keynes was rejected along with it. Similarly in economic theory, when economists looked back, not only were they unable to see past *The General Theory*'s characterization of "classical theory," but also the prevalence of the IS-LM model after the Second World War meant that even parts of *The General Theory* itself were obscured: Keynesian theory *had become* the IS-LM model. For economists of the 1970s, economic theorizing was mathematical modeling, and if they could not see a mathematical model, they could see only confusion.

In the 1990s and the years before the 2008 financial crisis, this was not obviously a problem (except for some historians who were troubled by the inconsistency of the myth with much of the evidence about Keynes). Bernanke's "Great Moderation"—an unparalleled decade of steady growth in North America and Europe—suggested that the economy was under control and the world did not need Keynesian policies. When the crisis hit, the inability to see the historical Keynes became a problem. It was not possible to return to the Keynesianism of the age of Keynes, for so much had changed; but the inability to see the historical Keynes hid from sight a Keynes who is far more relevant to the concerns that have emerged since the crisis.

3

KEYNES THE MORAL PHILOSOPHER

Confronting the Challenges to Capitalism

Capitalism in Question

Keynes was born, on June 5, 1883, into the Victorian era. It was close to seventy years since the end of the last major European war, and during this period the British economy had expanded enormously, Britain having become the workshop of the world. Britain was the center of the largest empire the world had ever seen—one on which the sun never set. It was an era of confidence, prosperity, and stability. During the Edwardian era, which began with Queen Victoria's death in 1901, seeds of change were sown: it saw the Boer War, suffragettes, the rise of the labor movement, and the constitutional crisis prompted by the "people's budget" of 1909—but the world remained a relatively calm and prosperous place. However, this peace and prosperity came to an abrupt end with the outbreak of the First World War, as Keynes entered his thirties. The unprecedented slaughter that took place on the battlefields of Belgium and France was enough, by itself, to undermine the optimism of the Victorian age, but the war also marked the transition to an age of economic chaos and political uncertainty. The war and the subsequent peace negotiations called into question the legitimacy of the old order: there were revolutions in Russia and Germany in which the tsar and the kaiser were overthrown. The profligate use of resources to execute the war, the unprecedented loss of human life, and the rapacious demands for reparations called into question the wisdom of political leaders on all sides. Following the war, socialist and later fascist parties became much more prominent in European parliaments.

The Bolshevik Revolution in Russia in 1917 had also raised the prospect of a new way of organizing society. The possibility of political change was no longer theoretical, but quite real. The overthrow of the kaiser and the instability of the Weimar Republic only increased the sense that the very form of society was in play. Undergirding all this political change were high levels of inflation across Europe during and after the war. By 1923 Germany was experiencing hyperinflation and rising unemployment. Britain avoided hyperinflation, but there were sharp changes in prices: they rose 50 percent in 1920 and a year later fell back to their previous level; after that, the problem was falling prices and, after 1924, persistent high unemployment. During the 1920s the United States avoided this chaos, enjoying unparalleled prosperity; but in 1929 the New York stock market collapsed, and after the global financial crisis of 1930 the entire world was dragged into the worst depression of all time. U.S. industrial production fell by 30 percent in two years, and unemployment rose to 25 percent by 1932. The depression affected the whole world. In 1932 unemployment reached 23 percent in Britain, 30 percent in Germany, 15 percent in France. Hitler's Nazis achieved power in 1933, and from 1936 to 1939 a bitter civil war was fought in Spain. World trade, and with it the world economy, collapsed. Meanwhile, though news was also emerging of Stalin's purges, sympathetic reporters, carefully chaperoned on tours of the Soviet Union, brought back reports of what the British socialist intellectuals Beatrice and Sidney Webb called "a new civilization."[1] Oswald Mosley's British fascists, influenced by developments in Italy and Germany, sought new ways of organizing society.

During the two decades that followed the First World War, capitalism did not perform well, and there was, more than at any time in its history, an open question whether it would survive. The relatively tranquil Victorian world that Keynes had been born into no longer existed. Trying to understand it and to remedy that broken world would become the central work of Keynes's life.

Keynes's Life

Keynes was born while W. E. Gladstone, the dominant figure in Victorian Liberalism, with its emphasis on free trade and fiscal rectitude, was prime minister. He came from an affluent family with strong Liberal roots, though at a time when the thinkers known as the "New Liberals" were beginning to move their party in a more collectivist direction, seeing economic activity as needing greater regulation than earlier generations of Liberals had contemplated. Keynes's paternal grandfather had been a self-made man whose fortune had come from creating hybrid flowers that were popular with English gardeners. His father, John Neville Keynes, had not entered the family business, instead embarking upon a highly successful academic career. He was among the first generation of those who trained formally in philosophy, but who went on to study economics as part of their specialization in logic and moral science. He lectured at Cambridge before entering university administration and becoming the Registrary, or top administrator, at Cambridge. Both Keynes's mother and father came from Nonconformist families, and his mother, Florence, became the first female mayor of Cambridge. They were great, representative Victorians, earnest and filled with a sense of civic duty, seeing themselves as having responsibility to improve society.

Keynes grew up in a comfortable middle-class home on Harvey Road in Cambridge, an affluent street not far from the university that dominated this medium-sized town. In a home adorned with William Morris wallpaper, he was raised like a hothouse flower to excel in his studies. He attended Eton, the most exclusive of Britain's private schools, and received a scholarship to enter Cambridge as a member of King's College. While at Cambridge, he studied mathematics and took a first-class degree in the subject, but he also began to build the life for which he would become famous. Straightaway, he was active in debate and was a vocal proponent of Liberal ideas, including free trade. He easily accepted his parents' Liberal Party politics.

He belonged to several clubs and societies while he was an undergraduate, of which the most important was the Cambridge Conversazione Society, known as the Apostles. This was an exclusive club that met on Saturday nights to hear a paper delivered by one of its members, followed by a discussion and a vote on a question raised by the paper that had been read. Past members who were still in Cambridge often attended the Saturday night meetings, and one of these was G. E. Moore, whose *Principia Ethica* was published in 1903 at the end of Keynes's first year at Cambridge. Keynes's contemporaries in the Apostles included several young men who, like himself, sought an escape from the ethos and mores of Victorian England.

When they graduated, several members of the Apostles, including Keynes, the biographer Lytton Strachey, and the novelist

E. M. Forster, moved to London, where they often congregated at the home of the recently deceased great Victorian intellectual Leslie Stephen. They became the male core of what came to be known, after the part of London in which they lived, as the Bloomsbury group. Fueled in part by Moore's argument that among the best things in life were art and friendship, Keynes and his friends formed a small, intimate coterie that explored both. It included Stephen's daughters the novelist Virginia Woolf and her sister, the painter Vanessa Bell, Duncan Grant, another painter, and the art critics Clive Bell and Roger Fry. There was also Leonard Woolf, political theorist and publisher. In their love of art and their friendship, they believed that they had found the best in life. In their art as well as in their private lives, they were rebelling against what they saw as the attitudes of their Victorian parents. It was Roger Fry, slightly older than the others, who had shocked London by mounting, in 1910, the first exhibition in which Post-Impressionists, including Cézanne, were shown in Britain. Strachey's *Eminent Victorians,* published in 1918 and taking on iconic figures such as Cardinal Manning and Florence Nightingale, sought to expose the hypocrisy of the older generation.

Keynes's degree was in mathematics (a degree in economics did not exist till 1903), so when he came to London, his formal instruction in economics consisted of a mere eight weeks, that being the time he had spent, after his graduation, studying with the great Cambridge economist Alfred Marshall to prepare for the Civil Service examination. (This pattern of studying mathematics and then "cramming" for the economics section of the civil service exam was not uncommon at this time.) Not surprisingly, as the son of a Cambridge economist he had already absorbed an unusual amount of the subject matter, and even before entering Cambridge he had known the philosopher-economist

Henry Sidgwick very well; he had worked as a proofreader for the 1901 edition of Sidgwick's textbook on economics. Despite the brevity of his formal training in economics, Keynes achieved second place in the Civil Service examination, and this result landed him a position in the India Office, where much of his brief included economic matters. His prowess at economics soon became clear to his superiors, and he quickly became an expert on the Indian monetary system.

However, Keynes did not stay in the Civil Service for long. In 1908 he took the risky decision to resign in order to take an insecure position lecturing at Cambridge, where his salary was paid by Marshall, who was due to retire a year later. His academic position became much more secure the following year, when he was elected a fellow of King's College. There followed the only period of his life when Keynes worked as a full-time academic. This ended with the First World War. The outbreak of war led to a financial crisis as several European stock exchanges closed, threatening the liquidity of the British banking system. The government needed to decide how to manage its gold reserves, and Keynes was asked for advice by his successor in the India Office. A year later, in 1915, he entered the Treasury, as assistant to the special adviser to David Lloyd George, who was to become prime minister in 1916, a position that incidentally exempted him from military service when conscription was introduced. At the Treasury he gained increasing responsibility, especially in relation to financing the war, and was eventually named as part of the negotiating team that was sent to the peace conference at Versailles. Here he became increasingly disillusioned with the demands for reparations being placed on Germany, which he saw as unethical and unrealistic, and he eventually resigned in protest. He wrote up his views in *The Economic Consequences of the Peace* (1919).

This book was crucial to Keynes's career and to the unusual position from which he was to write about capitalism for the rest of his life. It became a best-seller, with two important consequences: he became a celebrity whose views would be sought on economic matters, and the book launched him on a highly successful career in journalism. The unusual terms he had negotiated with his publisher (he was more confident about sales, so chose to bear the risk in exchange for keeping the profits earned by the book, the publisher receiving only a commission) meant that the book's runaway success gave him enough capital to set up as an investor, focusing initially on foreign-currency speculation (recall that it was his expertise in international finance, gained largely through his years in the India Office, that had brought him back into government in 1914). He made the decision not to return to being a full-time academic, but to support himself through his work in the City and his journalism, the latter being crucial on occasions when he got his fingers burned in speculative activity. He continued to lecture at Cambridge, but merely a series of eight lectures each year; he acted as bursar of King's College, remained editor of the *Economic Journal* (Britain's leading academic economics periodical), eventually settling into a routine of weekdays in London, weekends in Cambridge, and vacations (for writing) in his house in the Sussex countryside.

Keynes's writings on capitalism thus came from someone who was not a conventional academic, but who was actively involved in the City and financial markets (he also became director of an insurance company) and who, as a journalist, was continually engaging with issues of the moment at a time of economic and political turmoil. Yet he was also, through his connection with Cambridge, at the heart of the academic establishment. As regards government, he was now an outsider, his *Economic Consequences of the Peace* having alienated many in power. In the introduction to his *Essays in Persuasion* (1931), he described his own role as that of a Cassandra, identifying problems that others did not want to face; he was also notorious as someone who was willing to name those responsible for policy mistakes, as in his denunciation of the return to the gold standard in 1925, titled *The Economic Consequences of Mr Churchill.* However, despite being an outsider, he was never far from those in power. As had happened in the 1914 financial crisis, when he had something to say on an urgent issue, he knew who would want to hear his views and would take them up within the government.

But as befits an Apostle who became a founding member of Bloomsbury, Keynes had quickly become engaged in the emerging questions of the *nature* of the capitalism in which he lived. As a student, in his early efforts for the Liberal Club at Cambridge, Keynes had readily accepted capitalism as a form of organizing economic life. He debated questions about tariffs and free trade, for instance, which propelled him into the main economic policy questions of the day; but these were policy questions about how best to organize capitalism, not questions about whether capitalism itself was the right system.

Keynes's first significant published evaluation of capitalism, in the opening chapters of *The Economic Consequences of the Peace,* reflected both questions that were emerging in society at large concerning the legitimacy of capitalism and his own background in moral philosophy. In these chapters, Keynes looked carefully at the cultural assumptions that underpinned capitalism's rise in the nineteenth century and wondered whether the postwar European social psychology was capable of sustaining these assumptions. His only firm conclusions were that capitalism was based on shaky foundations and would require a new grounding if it were to survive. In the mid-1920s he sketched the outline for a book on capitalism, but never wrote it. But in essays he wrote in the 1920s and 1930s he developed many of the themes that he had broached in 1919 and would have covered in this book.

What Was Capitalism?

Like most economists who have written about capitalist economies, Keynes never offered a definition of capitalism; but the observations he made about it in the course of writing on other topics reveal a view of capitalism that is significantly different from that held by the economist who has probably been the most prominent exponent of capitalism in the past half-century, Milton Friedman. In his classic *Capitalism and Freedom* (1962), Friedman provided a series of studies of different markets, but, despite using the word "capitalism" in his title, he failed to offer any overarching analysis of the institutions that underpin capitalism or of the social conditions that are necessary for its functioning. Friedman seems to imply that capitalism requires private property and unfettered markets but nothing else. In contrast, for Keynes, capitalism was based around institutions that had evolved over a long period; it was not an idealized system consisting solely of individuals trying to maximize their own well-being and the markets created by these activities. Moreover, as far as Keynes was concerned, capitalism was still changing. One reason for his rejection of Marx was that he believed that capitalism had changed beyond recognition since the time when Marx observed it. Throughout his career Keynes held that capitalism was an imperfect machine that needed to be maintained and updated if it were to continue to work to meet society's needs.

The adjective Keynes most frequently used to qualify the word capitalism was "individualistic." However, by this he clearly did not have in mind a system, like Friedman's, that consisted of nothing other than individuals maximizing their own well-being and firms maximizing their own profits, operating in completely competitive markets. It was a much more complex system comprising the entire set of institutions, including government, governing economic activity. It made a difference who ran the system, for it needed to be run, whether by businessmen or politicians. Collective action could be part of capitalism: in fact, it might be through collective action that the institutions of capitalism would be improved.[2] Though he felt that Communism had failed, he was less dismissive of socialism; rather the problem was that, once socialism was instituted, he thought that people would lose interest in it, and the common purpose needed to hold society together would disappear. "Unless men are united by a common aim or moved by objective principles, each one's hand will be against the rest and the unregulated pursuit of individual advantage may soon destroy the whole. There has been no common purpose lately between nations or between classes, except for war."[3] There was no suggestion in Keynes's writing that unregulated capitalism was sufficient to reconcile the conflicting goals of individuals who had no common purpose. Perhaps this view is why Keynes, around this time, took an interest in nonprofit enterprises. It certainly explains why he believed that regulation was an integral part of a workable capitalism.

The essential feature of capitalism was, Keynes argued, "the dependence upon an intense appeal to the money-making and money-loving instincts of individuals as the main motive force of the economic machine."[4] But this did not imply that the agents operating under capitalism were selfish optimizers. Keynes, of course, had powerful theoretical reasons for not believing that behavior could be characterized in terms of rational agents taking optimal decisions. The theory of uncertainty that he had proposed in the dissertation he submitted to get his fellowship at King's College in 1908, and which he eventually published as *A Treatise on Probability* in 1921, rested on the assumption that the information necessary to make decisions in the way suggested by traditional economic theory was simply impossible to obtain. He preferred to reason on the basis of his own observations about how people actually behaved. But even beyond these observations about how people actually made their economic decisions, there was always the question for him of how people's moral judgments affected their behavior. Following his Cambridge mentor G. E. Moore, Keynes steadfastly refused to limit human behavior to utility maximizing. Like Moore, he believed that people were often motivated by a higher principle. Thus, when he wrote of "egotistic capitalism" and of "self-interested capitalists," he did so critically:[5] egotism and the pursuit of pure self-interest were linked to the system's failing to perform as it should. To explain how capitalism operated, it was also necessary to take account of moral judgments and how they changed.

The Fragility of Capitalism

Keynes did not see capitalism as a stable system. His *Economic Consequences of the Peace* (1919) was renowned for its critique of the era before 1914, expressed at the start of the first chapter. "Very few of us realise with conviction the intensely unusual, unstable, complicated, unreliable, temporary nature of the economic organisation by which Western Europe has lived for the last half century. We assume some of the most peculiar and temporary of our late advantages as natural, permanent, and to be depended on, and we lay our plans accordingly."[6] This was an integral part of his assault on the idea that it was possible to restore the old regime: that regime had been unstable and could not provide the security and stability for which people were yearning after the chaos of war and postwar economic dislocation. Savings lay at the heart of the problem, for Keynes saw society as being organized so as to promote capital accumulation and economic growth. His tone was almost Marxian when he wrote, "The duty of 'saving' became nine-tenths of virtue and the growth of the cake was the object of true religion."[7] Victorian and Edwardian society had been obsessed with saving in order to accumulate wealth. However, the system was tied up with the class structure of society, and the different sets of illusions held by each class created an unsustainable package. These are explained in a passage where Keynes's tone moves beyond one reminiscent of Marxism to a more complex social psychology of class.

> [T]he principle of accumulation based on inequality was a vital part of the pre-war order of society and of progress as we then understood it . . . and this principle depended on unstable psychological conditions, which it may be impossible to re-create. It was not natural for a population, of whom so few enjoyed the comforts of life, to accumulate so hugely. The war has disclosed the possibility of consumption to all and the vanity of abstinence to many. Thus the bluff is discovered; the labouring classes may be no longer willing to forgo so largely, and the capitalist classes, no longer confident of the future, may seek to enjoy

> more fully their liberties of consumption so long as they last, and thus precipitate the hour of their confiscation.[8]

The stability of the prewar era, as Keynes saw it, had rested on the necessity of both the working class and the capitalists living frugal lives: the workers had believed that it would be only after many generations that income would increase enough for their descendants to have the possibility of better material lives, while the capitalists had been content to save and live frugally in order to provide themselves with a justification for their claims to profit. In other words, the workers had believed that the system could not provide vastly greater resources in the present; the capitalists had accepted their slowly growing wealth as a necessary behavior to justify their privilege. But the war had shattered the social psychology of both classes. Working-class expectations had risen, and capitalist confidence had been shattered, making the old order impossible. It had been an equilibrium based on a bluff.

Keynes took up this idea that capitalism rested on a psychological equilibrium in *A Tract on Monetary Reform* (1923). The book was dedicated to the officials of the Bank of England, in the hope that they might be persuaded to conduct monetary policy on lines that were very different from those being pursued. As we shall see later on, Keynes constructed a technical argument about monetary policy using tools he had learned from his fellow Cambridge economists, but he also used the book to develop his own idea that capitalism depended on a social psychological equilibrium. He explained the motivations involved in the following way:

> No man of spirit will consent to remain poor if he believes his betters to have gained their goods by lucky gambling. To convert

> the business man into the profiteer is to strike a blow at capitalism, because it destroys the psychological equilibrium which permits the perpetuance of unequal rewards. The economic doctrine of normal profits, vaguely apprehended by everyone, is a necessary condition for the justification of capitalism. The business man is only tolerable so long as his gains can be held to bear some relation to what, roughly and in some sense, his activities have contributed to society.[9]

This passage is important because it goes beyond accounting for the exceptional circumstances of the prewar era, and offers a reason why capitalism cannot mean simply the unconstrained pursuit of profit (why capitalists cannot be pure profit maximizers). If rewards are unequal, they must be perceived to have some justification. In a society of gamblers, where gains are seen as unconnected with any notion of what people deserve to receive, capitalist arrangements come under threat. When writing about Russia in the mid-1920s, Keynes opined that if, as he believed had happened by then, capitalism became simply "a mere congeries of possessors and pursuers" (he does not use the phrase here, but this could be called egotistic or self-interested capitalism), people would find it morally unacceptable, and it would be threatened.[10] Under such circumstances, something more, such as great material success, was needed to hold it together: capitalism had to be "many times as efficient" as Communism simply to survive.[11]

Though Keynes wrote about the fragility of capitalism when thinking about the Communist alternative, the issue also arose in more narrowly economic discussions. Stability of the value of money was important, for this was central to the saving that lay at the heart of capitalism. In a sentence later quoted by Friedman, Keynes wrote, "Lenin is said to have declared that the best way to destroy the capitalist system was to debauch its currency," for changes in the value of money amounted to arbitrary confiscation of wealth.[12] Changes in the value of money exacerbated popular discontent concerning profiteering and the way people could accumulate wealth without doing anything to deserve it.[13] Persistent inflation would be tolerable only under "socialistic control."[14] Price changes, especially downward, could shake the foundations of capitalist society.[15]

The need for a set of beliefs that could convince people that capitalism was just also arose in Keynes's discussions of international relations. As his own investment activities spread into stocks and bonds from around the world in the 1920s, his understanding of international finance became even more astute. He wrote, in 1919, that the system whereby countries such as Argentina accumulated large debts to Europe, and continued to repay those debts, was fragile: "it has survived only because the burden on the paying countries has not so far been oppressive," because it corresponded to "real assets," and because past loans were smaller than intended future ones.[16] Each one of these three conditions was potentially problematic. The reference to "real assets" echoed Keynes's belief, discussed above, that wealth achieved by speculation and profiteering was widely unacceptable, and hence a danger for capitalism. But above all the problem was greed, for this could lead to burdens becoming intolerable. When negotiations over loans to Austria were dragging on into 1923 (and discussions of postwar debt continued much longer than this), Keynes used some of his most colorful language to denounce what was going on.

> Was ever a greater curse invented in the name of justice?—this doctrine that it is positively our moral duty to ruin ourselves and our vanquished neighbours together, in an attempt to extract from them an enslaving tribute for a period of generations. One wonders sometimes why Socialists have not seized on the whole conception as the crowning crime of capitalism! Never before in history have the greediest conquerors or the most austere crusaders conceived such penalties and such shackles as we modern industrial nations have sought to fix, by a ghastly perversion of the notion of foreign investment, on whole peoples and unborn innocents.[17]

Here, Keynes combined a denunciation of the expediency of imposing large burdens on countries that cannot pay them with attacks on the injustice of doing so. It is their injustice, as much as their direct macroeconomic consequences, which render them dangerous. He continued with this double charge a decade later, arguing that not only was this "decadent international" capitalism not virtuous; it was not even successful.[18] Not for him the idea promoted by the great Victorian Liberal statesman Richard Cobden, that increased interdependence in the world economic system, involving "the penetration of a country's economic structure by the resources and influence of foreign capitalists" and dependence on policy decisions in foreign countries, automatically led to world peace.[19] Because the moral justification of international relations was crucial to their acceptability, increased interdependence could be a recipe for instability if it was seen as motivated by unjust passions.

But the morality that drove capitalism was not the only thing necessary for it to be successful; in order to survive, capitalism also needed to be materially successful, and to do this it had to grow continuously. In the prewar era, this growth had taken place because of a psychological configuration, involving a set of inconsistent expectations, unlikely to recur. In the *Treatise on Money* (1930),[20] Keynes added a further argument. He explained the rise and fall of Spain in the sixteenth and seventeenth centuries by linking it to the flow of treasure from the newly conquered lands in America. The flow of treasure from the Americas caused a monetary expansion in Spain, stimulating profits and output. When the inflow of treasure ceased, the process went into reverse, and the Spanish economy went into decline. Keynes went on to argue that something similar was true of British capitalism in the nineteenth century. "Much of the material progress of the nineteenth century might have been impossible without the artificial stimulus to capital accumulation afforded by the successive periods of boom."[21] Thus at a time when some of his contemporaries, most visibly Friedrich Hayek, were arguing that because speculative booms were unsustainable, they should be reined back by the monetary authorities, Keynes argued that even though they were unsustainable, they were essential to capitalism. In this, he was much closer to the idea of his Cambridge colleague Dennis Robertson, who had argued that a certain level of fluctuations was "appropriate," a normal feature of capitalism. There might be scope for policy to reduce excessive fluctuations caused by monetary factors, but such action would not eliminate the cycle altogether.[22]

The Morality of Capitalism

Keynes was not an outright critic of capitalism. He saw its virtues, and could be scathing about those who rejected it completely.

When, during the First World War, he encountered the argument that "in the New Germany of the twentieth century, power without consideration of profit is to make an end to that system of capitalism, which came over from England a hundred years ago," he characterized the idea as "a nightmare."[23] By 1923 he considered Communism to have been discredited by experience.[24] Thus, capitalism was essential. This view echoes a passage in the unpublished 1926 draft of a book he had proposed to write on capitalism, which picks up on the remark, quoted above, that capitalism needs to be more successful than Communism:

> Capitalism develops a situation in which it is *indispensable*. The distribution of economic forces and the mass of population becomes such that without the *efficiency* of capitalism there is social collapse. Thus an injury done to the capitalistic system does not and cannot have the effect of restoring the pre-capitalistic regime. Thus we are *caught*. We have a dilemma between a society which is (morally) objectionable in itself and an economic collapse.[25]

He could therefore totally repudiate Marxism, which was based on the belief that, once capitalism had achieved its task, it would be possible to create a socialist society in which capitalism had been abandoned.

This belief that capitalism was indispensable lasted throughout his life, as is shown by the letter he wrote to Hayek on June 28, 1944, in which he gave his response to Hayek's recently published book, *The Road to Serfdom*. By this time Keynes had a lifetime of successful investing behind him, having made three fortunes for himself (and having lost only two of them). His successes and failures had given him a keener understanding of capitalism. The passage most often quoted from his letter to

Hayek is his remark that "morally and philosophically I find myself in agreement with virtually the whole of it; and not only in agreement with it, but in a deeply moved agreement." What is less widely noted is that he went on to criticize "the tendency to disparage the profit motive while still depending on it and putting nothing in its place."[26] He then praised a passage in which Hayek had written:

> the deliberate disparagement of all activities involving economic risk and the moral opprobrium cast on the gains which make risks worth taking which only few can win . . . The younger generation of today has grown up in a world in which in school and press the spirit of commercial enterprise has been represented as disreputable and the making of profit as immoral . . . the daily experience of the University teacher leaves little doubt that as a result of anti-capitalist propaganda values have already altered far in advance of the change in institutions which has yet taken place in this country. The question is whether by changing our institutions to satisfy the new demands, we shall not unwittingly destroy values which we rate still higher.[27]

Keynes wrote that, while he would like to see this theme expanded, this assessment "could not be bettered." As Keynes put it in a letter to Josiah Wedgwood in 1943, he did not wish to get rid of "the existing political and social set-up."[28]

Yet Keynes's belief that capitalism was essential did not dull his criticism of it. As has been explained above, capitalism needed to be regulated, and though its essence was the pursuit of financial gain, the selfish pursuit of gain—egoistic capitalism—was a recipe for disaster. "We do not wish," he argued in 1933 in the depths of the Great Depression, "to be at the mercy of world forces working out, or trying to work out, some uniform equilibrium according to the ideal principles, if they can be called such, of *laissez-faire* capitalism."[29] Keynes would here appear to be questioning not simply whether individuals actually benefit from laissez-faire capitalism, but also the desirability of equilibrium. Unregulated capitalism did not lead to an ideal outcome. However, he opposed unregulated egotism not simply because of its consequences, but because it offended his sense of morality. In 1932, echoing the experience of the Great Crash, he stated in a BBC radio broadcast: "The spectacle of capitalists, striving to become liquid as it is politely called, that is to say pushing their friends and colleagues into the chilly stream, to be pushed in their turn by some yet more cautious fellow from behind, is not an edifying sight."[30] But his objection to capitalism as a mechanism went further, extending to the principle of valuing all things in terms of money, which he saw as fundamental to capitalism.

> The exploitation and incidental destruction of the divine gift of the public entertainer by prostituting it to the purposes of financial gain is one of the worser [*sic*] crimes of present-day capitalism . . . But anything would be better than the present system. The position of artists of all sorts is disastrous. The attitude of an artist to his work renders him exceptionally unsuited for financial contacts.[31]

Art was, without doubt, something of particular importance to Keynes. However, this quotation would appear to go beyond the argument that artists are a breed apart and incapable of dealing with money (a position to which he might have been entitled given his experiences managing the financial affairs of the London Artists' Association). If capitalism is guilty of crimes against the highest form of human activity—and for Keynes art *did* have this status—then it was a strong indictment. But in referring to the prostitution of the entertainer's talents, Keynes is arguing that the very process of valuing them and trading them is to risk devaluing them. Unless he is prepared to draw a watertight circle round art, it is hard to avoid the conclusion that the devaluing effects of the money motive will be more pervasive, even if its effects are less severe with regard to activities other than art. That Keynes thought the problem to be more pervasive than the world of art is confirmed by remarks he made eleven years earlier when discussing Soviet Communism.

> [I]t seems clearer every day that the moral problem of our age is concerned with the love of money, with the habitual appeal to the money motive in nine-tenths of the activities of life, with the universal striving after individual economic security as the prime object of endeavour, with the social approbation of money as the measure of constructive success, and with the social appeal to the hoarding instinct as the foundations of the necessary provision for the family and for the future.[32]

His later remarks about art explain what he might have meant here. On this occasion, however, he went on to draw an analogy with religion. People needed an ideal, and, traditional religions having lost their significance, Russian Communism might offer a clue as to where a new one might be found. A few years later, he was even more forceful in his condemnation of moneymaking as an end in itself. "The love of money as a possession . . . [is] a somewhat disgusting morbidity, one of those semi-criminal, semi-pathological propensities which one hands over with a shudder to the specialists in mental disease."[33] So, for Keynes, capitalism was emphatically not an end in itself. It was necessary for freedom, but the activities of a capitalist society were not themselves an essential part of what that freedom was about. If moneymaking became an end in itself, it would devalue more valuable activities such as art; it would become a religion of an unattractive type. Rather, the purpose of freedom was the pursuit of other ends, such as writing, painting, and scientific research, for which capitalism provided the means. However, even this situation posed a problem, namely the motivation for saving. Immediately before the passage just quoted, Keynes had written of a paradox concerning human motives. As often, he started from the disillusion with prewar hopes.

> We used to believe that modern capitalism was capable, not merely of maintaining the existing standards of life, but of leading us gradually into an economic paradise where we should be comparatively free from economic cares. Now we doubt whether the business man is leading us to a destination far better than our present place. Regarded as a means he is tolerable; regarded as an end he is not so satisfactory.[34]

Disillusionment with the hope that capitalism would lead us toward a worthwhile goal had exposed the question of whether it was desirable as an end in itself. It was not. From here, Keynes moved into a discussion of religion: if one believed in heaven, then capitalism was purely a means; if one believed in progress, then capitalism was also a means to an end. But there was also the case in which one believed neither in heaven nor in progress, with the consequence that economic activity had to become an end in itself. "If there is no moral objective in economic progress, then it follows that we must not sacrifice, even for a day, moral to material advantage—in other words, we may no longer keep business and religion in separate compartments of the soul."[35] Loss of faith in supernatural religion and loss of faith in progress led inexorably to material advantage being pursued at the expense of moral advantage, something that Keynes, who rejected the utilitarian criterion, could not endorse. As a nonutilitarian, Keynes refused to weigh the pleasures of material gain above a set of higher values; in and of themselves, the pleasures of materialism could not form a legitimate defense of capitalism. The problems Keynes identified concerning saving were not simply technical macroeconomic problems—coordination failures, to use modern jargon—but had origins in a crisis in morality. Confrontation with moral problems lay at the heart of understanding capitalism.

If capitalism, then, was unsatisfactory, creating high interest rates, inequality, unemployment, and unedifying behavior on the part of capitalists, what was the solution? Keynes's answer was to reinstate the idea of progress, arguing that if progress could be taken far enough, these evils would be ameliorated if not removed. This was the strategy he outlined in an essay written in 1930, when a global financial crisis was pushing the world into depression, with the self-explanatory title "Economic Possibilities for Our Grandchildren," and in the last chapter of *The General Theory*.[36] He speculated that mankind might be able to solve its economic problem and to get rid of the scarcity of capital goods.[37] Doing this would, he wrote, "rid us . . . of most of the evils of capitalism."[38] As capital ceased to be scarce, its price (the rate of interest) would fall toward zero, and as a result the rentier class would disappear—his famous "euthanasia of the rentier."[39] People could decide when to spend their income, but would not be rewarded for saving. Competition would be less intense as people stopped striving for wealth but sought to enjoy it. Artists, formerly prostituted under capitalism, would come into their own.

> Thus for the first time since his creation man will be faced with his real, his permanent problem—how to use his freedom from pressing economic cares, how to occupy the leisure, which science and compound interest will have won for him, to live wisely and agreeably and well . . . it will be those peoples, who can keep alive, and cultivate into fuller perfection, the art of life itself and do not sell themselves for the means of life, who will be able to enjoy the abundance when it comes.[40]

Capitalism could become free of its most objectionable features. However, even though the rate of profit would fall to zero, there would still be scope for enterprise: it would only be the rate of return on completely safe investments that would fall to zero, and positive returns would still be available to reward those who took risks.

Cultivating the Imaginative Life

The picture of capitalism that emerges from Keynes's scattered but consistent comments on the topic fits perfectly with the moral values that he developed first as a member of the Apostles and later as a member of Bloomsbury. It is impossible to understand his insistence on maintaining his own moral critique of capitalism without understanding his complex relationship to the friends and colleagues with whom he had developed his vision of the world as a young man. After all, the group remained central to his life until the end. The vision of the future with which Keynes ended his magnum opus, *The General Theory,* of a world in which material goods would cease to be scarce, effecting a revolution in society, was something he took from his Bloomsbury friends. Keynes argued in an autobiographical essay written in 1938, "My Early Beliefs," that not only had these old friends remained central to who he was, but that all of them remained under the sway of Moore's work, especially his antiutilitarian ethics.

But if utility or pleasure was not the highest human value, what was? In the much-cited closing chapter of *Principia Ethica,* Moore allowed that friendship and art were two things that almost always led to states of mind that could be described as good. Seen through this prism, it is not difficult to understand the very different attitude that Keynes held about capitalism, especially when compared to the attitude of more modern economists. When an economist like Friedman analyzes economic behavior, he imagines utility maximization to be the highest human value. Thus, if markets are allowed to operate unencumbered by either government interference or artificially constructed barriers (such as medical licensing), then the outcome must be the best possible one that can be attained. Where modern economists question that conclusion, they almost invariably do so by identifying market failures, not by questioning the notion that utility is what matters. For Keynes, on the other hand, there were higher values than utility maximization. And profit maximization could have no value except as a means to a higher end.

During the 1920s, when Keynes was developing his ideas about capitalism, he embraced not only the ethical critique of capitalism, but also the idea that people were motivated by something other than utility maximization. This perspective presaged much of what he would say in the 1930s about the fragility of capitalism. The conception that Keynes had of capitalism as a means to an end is also clarified by looking at how his Moorean values were cultivated and expanded through his friendship with Roger Fry, the art critic, and himself an Apostle from the early 1890s.[41] Trained in biology and a keen follower of Darwinian theory, Fry developed a conception of the world that involved two spheres of human experience: the "actual life" and the "imaginative life." The actual life involved all the necessary biological functions such as eating and procreation, while the imaginative life involved the arts, the pursuit of scientific knowledge, and creative writing. In Fry's scheme, it was clear that people would always have to meet their basic needs, but he believed that as they fulfilled those needs they would devote more and more of their resources to the pleasures of the imaginative life.

Here, in a tightly wrapped package, was a practical translation of Moore's values into everyday life. The highest human values were to be found in the pursuit of the arts, and the best company was the artist and critics who had come together to become Bloomsbury. There was no doubt that they needed to meet their basic human needs, but the highest value was on what they made together as occupants of the imaginative sphere of human existence. This stance provides a theoretical justification for Keynes's lifelong commitment to the arts. Aside from his personal investment in art and his support for artists, many of them his friends, through the London Artists' Association, he was instrumental in establishing the Cambridge Arts Theatre, the Camargo Society (which developed into the Royal Ballet), and above all the Arts Council of Great Britain, which, through serving as the prototype for similar organizations in other countries, helped change the relationship between society, government, and the arts in the Western world.

The means necessary to pursue the imaginative life looked to be best provided by capitalism. But capitalism was not itself the appropriate end. Fry had argued that the greatest impediment to correctly understanding and integrating the two spheres of human life was the drive for emulation, an idea he had taken from the famous critic of American society Thorstein Veblen. If one were always trying to acquire what others had, the pursuit of the imaginative life would be blocked. It is not difficult to see this attitude reflected in Keynes's statements about the love of money and unbridled greed. These attitudes represented a desire to have (or exceed) what others had and so stood as impediments to escaping from simple survival and achieving the imaginative life.

In addition to providing the moral values by which capitalism should be judged, Bloomsbury provided a perspective on human existence that meshed with Keynes's view of the fragility of capitalism and its psychological foundations. Inconsistent expectations and the tensions these created were a prominent Bloomsbury theme. "Much of the Bloomsbury literature and works of art, and indeed their style of life, was predicated on the presumption that personal, social, political, cultural, international and economic institutions inherited from the Victorian age were no longer able, if they ever had been, to resolve the destructive tensions resulting from inconsistent expectations."[42] The First World War offers the most obvious example. Keynes's analysis of prewar Victorian and Edwardian capitalism in *The Economic Consequences of the Peace* was another. So, too, were the dysfunctional families in the novels of E. M. Forster, David Garnett, and Virginia Woolf. Their response was to search for new solutions, whether in personal relationships or in national or international economic affairs.

> Instead of starting from the presumption that existing adjustment mechanisms would work, the Bloomsburys usually presumed

> just the opposite, and they looked immediately for alternatives. But to find satisfactory alternative mechanisms the biggest challenge, they discovered, was to change the basic psychological attitudes of actors as well as the institutions through which they interacted. To emerge from the Great Depression, Keynes suggested, one of the major challenges was to achieve "the readjustment of the habits and instincts of the ordinary man, bred into him for countless generations, which he may be asked to discard within a few decades."[43]

There are two themes here. One is the importance of psychology, again a feature of Bloomsbury novels as much as of Keynes's economic writing. Craufurd Goodwin draws attention to the need to change human habits and instincts, but there was also Keynes's emphasis on expectations: policy measures such as leaving the gold standard, or public-works expenditure worked as much by creating a climate of optimism as through their "mechanical" effects.

In the end, Keynes came to a position which seems perfectly reasonable for a moral philosopher, but which by modern standards for analyzing capitalism seems somewhat unusual. He saw capitalism as morally flawed because of its dependence on the moneymaking motive, but nonetheless saw it as the best alternative available. He believed that capitalism had always evolved and changed during human history, and so he believed that continued evolution was still possible. Unlike those defenders of capitalism today who argue vociferously that there is nothing wrong with it and that it is beyond criticism, or those for whom it a system beyond hope, Keynes took a critical position and demanded that the system's flaws be addressed frankly. Only by addressing the flaws honestly could the system be reformed enough to survive. In many ways, Keynes's life work can be best understood as having fully realized his own imaginative life by developing this understanding of capitalism and how and why to preserve it. To do this, however, he had to do more than provide a moral critique, or even a vision of how capitalism operated: he had to provide a theory of how a capitalist economy worked. It is to this that we now turn.

4

KEYNES THE PHYSICIAN

Developing a Theory of a Capitalist Economy

Interwar Fluctuations

Had Keynes been simply a philosopher who offered a moral critique of capitalism, his influence would have been a tiny fraction of what it was. His reputation arose because he developed a theory of how capitalist economies worked that could be used to explain why they had failed so catastrophically in the 1930s and what might be done about it. However, Keynes approached this task not as a conventional academic, writing learned tomes and articles in specialist journals aimed solely at his fellow economists, but also as a journalist and businessman. The financial success of *The Economic Consequences of the Peace* enabled him to support himself by his journalism, consultancy, and government advice while becoming, simultaneously, both one of the leading economic journalists of his generation and one of its leading academic economists. He remained a fellow of King's College, delivering a series of eight lectures each year, running a seminar for the faculty and selected students, and spending many years as the college's bursar, but he had no university appointment. (He never had the title of professor.) As a result, though he remained closely connected with his Cambridge colleagues, developing his ideas sometimes with them and sometimes in opposition to them, much of what he wrote on the economy was published in newspapers and magazines and in the very large number of reports and memoranda he produced in his capacity as an investor and as an expert advising the government.

Given that his academic work was inseparable from his journalism, it is therefore not surprising that he approached the economy as a physician, seeking to diagnose its problems and to propose remedies. This attitude lay, in varying degrees, behind the three major books in which he developed his analysis of capitalist economies: *A Tract on Monetary Reform* (1923), in which he first applied his intuitions about the potential instability of capitalism to the problem of monetary policy; *A Treatise on Money* (1930), in which he sought to consolidate his academic reputation by providing a novel theoretical framework for monetary policy; and *The General Theory of Employment, Interest and Money* (1936), which laid the theoretical foundations for the Keynesian economics that became the new economic orthodoxy for close to three decades after the Second World War.

In his initial work in economic theory, Keynes was somewhat conventional and followed closely in the theoretical footsteps of his teacher Alfred Marshall and Marshall's successor at Cambridge, A. C. Pigou. Through his work in the India Office, he established himself as an expert on international finance, specializing in relationships between Britain and India, then part of the British Empire, his first book being *Indian Currency and Finance* (1913). After the First World War, having long since left the India Office, he turned to the problems that the new world order was throwing up. The 1920s were a period of instability, with a short-lived boom in 1920, caused by businesses replenishing their stocks after the war, followed by an equally sudden collapse the following year. The big question, however, concerned the exchange rate, which during the war had been allowed to float free from its prewar value against gold and other currencies. The official policy, laid down in a Whitehall report of 1919, was that sterling should return to the gold standard at its prewar parity of £1 = $4.86. The price of £3 17s 10½d (£3.89 in modern money) per ounce of gold on which this parity was based had great symbolic importance, being the value of sterling established by Sir Isaac Newton in 1717, when he was master of the mint.

In the *Tract on Monetary Reform,* Keynes again dealt with exchange rates, but his largest concern was to address the immediate problems caused by the inflation that had followed the First World War. The postwar inflation caused obvious problems for people who tried to keep up with ever-rising prices and also had wreaked havoc on currency exchange rates. He hoped to find a way to stabilize prices and exchange rates. The fact that Keynes was focused on the problem of inflation in his first well-known book of monetary theory will surprise people who know only the caricature of Keynes propagated in the 1970s as someone who developed policies that cause inflation.

The *Tract* was based on two theories, both with long pedigrees. One was the Cambridge version of the quantity theory of money that Keynes had learned from his teacher Marshall and was also used by his colleague Pigou. This postulated a relationship between the amount of money in circulation and the price level; given the quantity of goods and services being produced, the more money in circulation, the higher the price level. Though the Cambridge economists emphasized the instability of this relationship, which would change over the business cycle as changes in output and expectations caused changes in the amount of money people wanted to hold, the quantity theory was the standard approach to analyzing inflation, at least since the time of David Hume in the 1750s.

The other theory, known as purchasing-power parity, was based on the observation that if goods can move freely between countries, they must sell at roughly the same price in all countries when they are converted into a common currency. Thus if coal sells for £10 per ton in Britain, and the exchange rate is $4.86 to £1, it must sell for $48.60 per ton in the United States. The relationship is far from precise, because it does not take into account transport costs, and because it should hold only in the long run, when traders have had time to respond to any unexpected price differences. But Keynes accepted it as a rough-and-ready guide to international price movements in composing the *Tract.*

In two chapters that Milton Friedman was later to praise, Keynes explained the evils that arose from inflation (rising prices) and deflation (falling prices). Inflation was unjust because it reduced the value of debts by redistributing wealth from the lender to the borrower; it amounted to a tax that had to be paid by anyone who had lent money to the government. Deflation was even worse because even the fear of falling prices was enough to inhibit business activity; falling prices meant that if entrepreneurs bought goods they would face the prospect of having to sell them later at lower prices. Using the quantity theory of money and purchasing-power parity, Keynes argued that the goal of British monetary policy should be to stabilize the price level, preventing either inflation or deflation, even if this meant that the exchange rate had to fluctuate. As he summed up his argument, "The individualistic capitalism of today . . . presumes a stable measuring-rod of value [i.e., price level], and cannot be efficient—perhaps even cannot survive—without one."[1]

Keynes's greatest hope was that he had found guidelines that the monetary authorities could follow in the absence of the gold standard. Stability in the price level did not require returning to the way monetary policy had been conducted for the past two hundred years. Indeed, returning to the gold standard would not generate the stability that people craved, for it would result in harmful changes in the price level because of the necessity to keep the exchange rate fixed. Although he had not strayed far from his Cambridge roots in his choice of the two theoretical models he used to build his argument, his advocacy of an activist policy, in which the central bank took responsibility for the price level, took him beyond anything Marshall or Pigou had advocated (though Marshall had been aware that some of his monetary proposals would require that the value of sterling in terms of other currencies would fluctuate). Indeed, his main point was not the detailed policy recommendations but the underlying view that the authorities should face up to the fact that the economy needed to be managed: it could not be left to its own devices.

> [W]e must free ourselves from the deep distrust which exists against allowing the regulation of the standard of value [the price level] to be the subject of *deliberate decision*. We can no longer afford to leave it in the category of which the distinguishing characteristics are possessed in different degrees by the weather, the birth rate, and the Constitution—matters which are settled by natural causes, or are the resultant of the separate action of many individuals acting independently, or require a revolution to change them.[2]

The break with his predecessors, who had focused on rules rather than active management of the economy, is not surprising given his belief that capitalism was inherently unstable. Writing after the First World War had shattered the illusion that capitalism was inherently stable, Keynes had made a further step to analyze what caused that instability and how to mitigate it.

Though it did not break new theoretical ground, his analysis in the *Tract* lay beneath another of his more polemical works, *The Economic Consequences of Mr Churchill,* published two years later. The politician responsible for returning Britain to the gold standard at the old parity of £1 = $4.86 was Winston Churchill, once the reforming Liberal politician who, together with the Welsh firebrand David Lloyd George, had been a member of the prewar Liberal government that provoked a constitutional crisis by raising taxes to pay for social reforms, but was now chancellor of the Exchequer in a Conservative government. In his new position, Churchill was responsible for the decision to put Britain back on the gold standard. However, whereas the official view was that British prices were merely 2.5 percent higher than U.S. prices, Keynes argued that the gap was 10 percent, which would mean that wages had to fall much further to accommodate a return to the gold standard at the old exchange rate, creating severe problems for the British economy. Keynes argued that Churchill was inflicting great damage on the economy by favoring stability of the exchange rate over stability of the internal price level. His real fear was that a stable exchange rate might lead to an unstable economy.

Stagnation in the British Economy

By the end of the 1920s, under the restored gold standard, Britain's economic problems were no longer inflation and exchange rate volatility but persistent deflation and stagnation, concentrated in the export industries: the old staples of textiles, coal mining, iron and steel, and shipbuilding. Throughout the 1920s, when the United States was enjoying the prosperity that made the crash of 1929 so traumatic, Britain was stagnating. The attempt to keep industry competitive called for cuts in wages, which provoked a bitter miners' strike. Support for the miners erupted into a general strike in 1926, which polarized the country as the army was brought in and managers had to keep public transport going. Being a political realist, Keynes realized that though the cause of these problems might be an overvalued currency, as he had argued in his essay on Churchill, there was no longer any point in challenging the gold standard. The problems had changed, and so the physician needed new tools to diagnose them correctly.

The 1920s were a time of change in Keynes's life. In addition to establishing himself as a leading economic journalist, he began to manage the investments of King's College. He had begun to trade on his own account in 1919 (initially in the markets for foreign currency), and in the 1920s he began to work as an investment adviser to others. In 1921 he became the chairman of the National Mutual Insurance Company, and in 1923 he helped to put together a group of investors to take control of the old Liberal magazine *The Nation*.

He also surprised his family and friends by marrying the noted Russian ballerina Lydia Lopokova. Since his time at Cambridge as an undergraduate, Keynes had been a practicing homosexual, but after watching Lopokova, whom he had first met in 1919, perform in 1922, he fell madly in love with her, and they married on August 4, 1925. This, together with the fact that Lydia was uneducated and was an outsider in the highly intellectual Bloomsbury environment, created tension in his relationships with his old friends in Bloomsbury; but the marriage provided Keynes with a real sense of joy and contentment.

Keynes continued to gain a higher profile throughout the 1920s, and by the end of 1930 he had become an adviser to the government in two different capacities: as a member of the Macmillan Committee, set up by the chancellor of the Exchequer to examine the causes of (and possible cures for) Britain's economic recession; and as a member of the Economic Advisory Council, set up by the prime minister to advise the government. Now Keynes was in a much better position to be heard.

But these new public positions may not have put him in a better position to develop the diagnostic tools he sought. By 1929, when he was appointed to the Macmillan Committee, Keynes had already been working on the *Treatise on Money* for five years. During 1929 and 1930, when he was appointed to the Economic Advisory Council, he used both venues to test his evolving ideas. The effects on his writing were not good, however. Instead of causing him to sharpen his arguments, his efforts to use his theoretical innovations as debating tools left him unsatisfied. On the day that he sent the book to the printers, he wrote his mother and told her that the book was an "artistic failure."[3] In part because he had been rushed and busy, and in part because Keynes had tried to claim too much for his work, he was left with a product that did not please him.

Another interesting result of his attempt to use his new ideas in discussions over policy is that we can see how far he had strayed, in the *Treatise on Money,* from his roots in the Cambridge theories of money and the trade cycle. In the traditional Cambridge theory of the trade cycle, shifts in the outlook of investors between optimism and pessimism were taken to be the primary force driving the economy up and down. Keynes himself had embraced this theory early in his career, but in the *Treatise* he had dismissed it completely and utterly. In its place, he had substituted a theory of the trade cycle that identified interest rates as the primary cause, together with a new theoretical framework to replace the old quantity theory. This change, which in retrospect appears a detour, can be linked to his involvement in policy debates while he was working on the *Treatise.*

When Pigou, as the professor of economics at Cambridge, gave evidence to the Macmillan Committee in 1930, Keynes treated him as if he were in the dock answering for his analytical errors. Pigou's testimony was based on the theory that expectations of future profits played a major role in determining investment. In cross-examining him, Keynes tried to get Pigou to change his mind: he pushed him to admit that the cause of the falling investment that had caused the Depression was the high rates of interest that the Bank of England was required to maintain in order to keep Britain on the gold standard, and nothing else. This was Keynes's own view. Thus, just after Pigou had stated that falling investment was a major cause of Britain's current troubles, Keynes tried to corner him into agreeing with his own diagnosis of the problem.

> *Keynes:* Does this [investment] not depend on the rate of interest?
>
> *Pigou:* Undoubtedly, in part.
>
> *Keynes:* Is not that fundamental?
>
> *Pigou:* There is the state of mind of the business man. The business man might be in such a state that he would not borrow money or use money at 0 percent.
>
> *Keynes:* That is an extremely abnormal state of things?
>
> *Pigou:* It is the two things—interest and his state of mind.[4]

Pigou refused to accept Keynes's claim that the state of mind of businessmen had nothing to do with investment. Keynes's position here amounted to a denial not just of the theory he had previously supported, but also of the position he was later to take in *The General Theory.*

This exchange nicely illustrates the problem that Keynes was encountering in trying to bring the *Treatise on Money* to fruition while simultaneously serving as a consultant to the government. In order to be effective in his new role, Keynes felt that he needed to identify a clear cause of the country's economic maladies so that he could, likewise, identify a clear solution. In his mind, the problem was interest-rate policy, and to make that case he ruled out any important role for other factors. His approach reflected a thoroughly realistic view about how politics worked. However, this pragmatic approach to identifying a cause and a cure for Britain's economic problems, and then focusing on it to the exclusion of all other factors, did not serve him well as a theorist. The result is that in the *Treatise on Money* Keynes adopted what has been insightfully described as a "magic formula mentality."[5]

The simple, mechanical nature of Keynes's approach in the *Treatise* is explicit in his central innovation: the portentous "fundamental equations." Though he describes them as "fundamental," they involve only elementary manipulations of some basic accounting identities and represent another version of the quantity theory of money that Keynes had used in the *Tract.* His derivation of the equations is certainly novel, but as in the case of the *Tract,* though Keynes was able to apply them with great insight as a diagnostic tool, they had great limitations as an economic theory.

When compared with the *Tract,* Keynes's innovation in the *Treatise* was to analyze the economy in terms of the relationship between savings and investment. If the economy is to prosper, savings must find their way, through the financial system, into the hands of businessmen who will invest the money in productive assets (buildings, machinery, and other capital goods). If, as Keynes was arguing, this is not happening and the resulting lack of investment is causing a depression, then it is incumbent on the economic theorist to understand why people save, why they invest, and hence why the savings are not being turned into investments during a downturn. As his exchange with Pigou makes clear, Keynes's answer was the interest rate. If the interest rate is too high, savers will be induced to save a lot, but, on the other hand, businessmen will be less inclined to borrow and take the risk of investing in new capital goods.

Using this simple theory, Keynes identified what he called, following the Swedish economist Knut Wicksell, a "natural" rate of interest that would equilibrate the level of savings and the level of investment. The problem facing the British economy in 1930 was that, in order to remain on the gold standard, with sterling at its historic value in terms of gold and the U.S. dollar, the authorities had to keep the rate of interest above this natural rate, causing investment to fall short of savings. The obvious remedy, of course, was to abandon the gold standard, but Keynes realized that, politically, this move was unrealistic. As a result he had to search for short-run palliatives that could stimulate the economy, such as tariffs to limit imports or public-works projects. Nonetheless, the fundamental problem was that interest rates were too high.

The Great Depression

Keynes judged his own work according to very high standards, and he was aware that there were problems with the way he had expounded his ideas in the *Treatise.* However, his belief that the book was a failure had deeper roots. The book's lukewarm reception indicated that it was not the definitive statement of monetary economics that he had hoped to achieve. Even more important, though the book was published in 1930, after the stock-market crash and as the world was plunging into the Great Depression, the *Treatise* still reflected the concerns of the late 1920s and not the rapidly emerging problem of worldwide mass unemployment. This new problem brought into sharp focus the limitations of the theory he was proposing.

When he discussed his intellectual journey toward *The General Theory,* Keynes reported that, shortly after the *Treatise* was published, his younger colleagues at Cambridge made him realize that he had been trying to discover how to get an economy back to full employment using a theory that could not explain the level of output and employment. *The General Theory* was the result of his search for a theory that could explain how output could settle down at different levels and therefore be something that government policy could change. However, though it was true that the *Treatise* did not have a good explanation of the level of output, there was a deeper problem with the book. In it, despite his efforts at novelty, Keynes was still working with older theoretical constructs. As in the *Tract,* he went some way beyond his Cambridge colleagues in arguing that the authorities should adopt a more active approach to policymaking, taking deliberate decisions about what the price level should be, a position that brought him some notoriety. But although he was looking for new tools with which to make better diagnoses and propose better remedies, his approach had become more one-dimensional and less flexible. He had, indeed, adopted a "magic formula mentality," for his so-called fundamental equations provided a mechanical connection between monetary policy and the level of prices. The book did offer a detailed analysis of financial markets, but this played only a minor role in his central argument; had Keynes paid more attention to his own more subtle discussions of investors' behavior he could not have questioned Pigou in the way that he did.

In the years from 1930 to 1936, Keynes went on to develop a theory about how the level of employment was determined, but in doing this he also moved away from his magic-formula mentality, writing a book in which the theory was more complex than the processes he could capture in his equations. He developed an integrated theory of how disturbances in financial markets could disrupt the production of goods and services, which was centered on the insight, missing from the *Treatise,* that a capitalist economy could get shunted into a position in which it had high unemployment without any tendency to recover toward full employment. This, of course, reflected the reality on both sides of the Atlantic in 1931 when Keynes started working on *The General Theory.* Not only was Britain by then in its eighth consecutive year of very high unemployment, but there had been a worldwide collapse in output and employment, with output in the United States falling by a third between 1929 and 1933. In 1930 there had been no satisfactory theory about how the economy could move into a deep depression and stay there, but by the time *The General Theory* had appeared, such a theory had become essential.

In showing that the economy could get stuck in a deep depression, Keynes likened himself to the famous nineteenth-century economist Robert Malthus (more famous for his theory of population), who, writing in the 1820s, shortly after the Napoleonic Wars, had argued a similar point against his friend and theoretical adversary David Ricardo. Ricardo was a proponent of what Keynes termed "Say's Law," named after Ricardo's contemporary, the French economist Jean-Baptiste Say, which could be summed up as "supply creates its own demand." The key idea was that producing goods worth $100 creates incomes exactly equal to $100, for anything that is not paid out in wages to workers or to the owners of land and natural resources is profit, the income received by capitalists. Thus, provided that any money that is saved is channeled, via the financial system, to businessmen who will invest it in capital goods, there can be no shortage of demand as a whole. There may be insufficient demand for particular goods (businesses will make mistakes all the time), but there cannot be what Malthus and his contemporaries called a "general glut." Malthus argued that Say's Law was wrong, and that it was possible for an economy to get stuck indefinitely in a position in which large parts of the population could not find regular work. Keynes's embrace of Malthus, whose ideas were pointed out to him shortly after he had begun thinking in this way, was all the sweeter for him because Malthus had been a Cambridge man, allowing him to portray Malthus as an early Cambridge economist.

Keynes thus placed himself in a long line of debate about the question of *how* capitalism works. In that sense, he was not doing anything new. Neither was he the first person to theorize about how the economy as a whole works. There were many prominent economists in the first three decades of the twentieth century who had worked this field, theorizing about the financial system, how money and credit worked, and how the business cycle functioned. Keynes did not invent macroeconomics: indeed, as his own invocation of Malthus and Ricardo suggested, he had many predecessors in the nineteenth century. What was novel about *The General Theory* was Keynes's success in creating a theory that explained the level of output and showed how a shortage of aggregate demand might cause the level of output to be too low for workers to be fully employed.

Another way of understanding Keynes's achievement in developing a theory of how output and employment could change is to note that it meant that he finally had to abandon the quantity theory of money. While he had been able to underpin his work in both the *Tract* and the *Treatise* with variations on the quantity theory, as he came to attach more importance to the fact that the amount of money people hold (whether as currency or in bank accounts) will depend on expectations about the future and can easily change, he needed a different explanation of how much people will choose to spend. He had begun to move in this direction in the *Treatise,* with its discussions of saving and investment, but in *The General Theory* he went a stage further. Spending was taken to depend on income, which in turn depended on the level of output, and the quantity of money played a minor role, being no more than one of the factors lying behind the rate of interest. Thus, one of the results of Keynes's work on *The General Theory* was that he had to move beyond one of the common frameworks in the 1920s and 1930s for analyzing the business cycle, the quantity theory of money, and develop a new set of tools for analyzing how a monetary economy worked.

Keynes described *The General Theory* as a work of economic theory addressed to his fellow economists. Even if this helps explain why there is not more on policy, it remains surprising how little the book said about how the government should fight mass unemployment. This was a subject on which he already had a reputation, for during the 1920s he had become a well-known advocate of using public-works projects (spending on roads, schools, hospitals, and other forms of public investment) to stimulate the economy. Together with a young economist, Hubert Henderson, he had contributed to the 1929 general election campaign with a widely circulated campaign manifesto titled *Can Lloyd George Do It?* Lloyd George, leader of what remained of the Liberal Party, was proposing to spend £250 million on public-works projects in order to drive the unemployment rate down. Keynes and Henderson argued that this would work. It was well known that such spending would raise incomes, and that when people spent those incomes, spending would rise further. But they had no way to work out *how* this rise in public-works spending would raise output.

By 1933, when Keynes produced a pamphlet (or rather two pamphlets, for the British and American editions were different), based on four pieces in *The Times,* titled *The Means to Prosperity,* this problem had been solved. In this pamphlet Keynes used, for the first time, the device of the "multiplier," worked out by his young Cambridge colleague Richard Kahn and published in 1931 in the *Economic Journal,* which Keynes edited. This theory shows that, if $100 in spending creates incomes that generate a further $50 in spending, and that $50 generates a further $25, and so on, the net result will be that output rises by a total of $200. In this case, the multiplier is two, meaning that the rise in output will be twice as large as the rise in public-works expenditure.

This pamphlet stands midway between the *Treatise* and *The General Theory* in terms of its analysis. The foreshadowing of *The General Theory* is clear in that *The Means to Prosperity* contains the Kahn multiplier, demonstrating that Keynes was beginning to work out ways in which he could explain the level of output, something that he had failed to do in the *Treatise.* However, in many ways the pamphlet still shows Keynes in the mind-set of the *Treatise*. For instance, it contains a thorough discussion of monetary policy and an explanation of why it is important for the central bank to lower interest rates to stimulate private investment in order to return the economy to health. But there is still no attention paid to the role of what Pigou had called the "state of mind of the business man." Keynes's failure to see at this point the possibility that the low level of investment might be caused by something other than interest rates being too high left him in the throes of his magic-formula mentality, albeit using Kahn's multiplier deftly in order to make what appears to be an airtight argument for a public-works stimulus. He still seemed to want a simple answer for a complex problem. But it would be the last instance in which he would fully employ the magic-formula mentality.

The General Theory

In manifestos such as *Can Lloyd George Do It?* and pamphlets such as *The Means to Prosperity,* Keynes advocated the use of public-works projects as a cure for stagnation and unemployment. *The General Theory* certainly does not disavow such policies, but it strikes a more cautious note, for Keynes by then recognized that such a policy might not work if it caused capitalists to get cold feet and curtail their investment expenditures, offsetting the stimulus arising from the public works. In the three years between the publication of *The Means to Prosperity* and *The General Theory,* Keynes had come to see that there was perhaps no magic formula that would easily guarantee recovery and, though he was now using a new theory, had thereby returned to the more subtle and pragmatic approach of the Cambridge tradition. While he had great confidence in the essentials of his theory, he was less certain about the policy conclusions that should be drawn from it. Thus when he defended *The General Theory* in 1937, after explaining that he had provided a theory of why output and employment were liable to fluctuate, he went on to say:

> It does not offer a ready-made remedy as to how to avoid these fluctuations and to maintain output at a steady optimum level . . . Naturally I am interested not only in the diagnosis, but also in the cure; and many pages of my book are devoted to the latter. But I consider that my suggestions for a cure, which, avowedly, are not worked out completely, are on a different plane from the diagnosis. They are not meant to be definitive; they are subject to all sorts of special assumptions and are necessarily related to the particular conditions of the time.[6]

This move away from the magic-formula mentality took the form of a changed attitude toward the "state of mind of the business man," which had come in the autumn of 1933, a few months after he published *The Means to Prosperity*. We do not know what finally tipped the balance for him, but it might well have been the failure of *The Means to Prosperity* to persuade the authorities to undertake large-scale public-works projects. His failure to influence policy in Britain may not have been too surprising, for the National Government, formed in 1931 as an alliance of Labour and the Conservatives and led by Labour's Ramsey MacDonald, was fiscally conservative and was not likely to adopt the polices that he and Hubert Henderson had advocated for the Liberals in 1929. But his failure to influence the recently elected Franklin Roosevelt in the United States was certainly a disappointment. The inauguration of Roosevelt's New Deal was an excellent chance to introduce bold new ideas, but when Roosevelt, who had run on a campaign to balance the budget, introduced the New Deal in 1933 it contained no mention of public-works projects or government budget deficits. Keynes's disappointment may have been all the greater if, as has been argued, it was Roosevelt's statement, to the American people, that "we have nothing to fear but fear itself" that had stimulated his belief in the centrality of expectations to the problem of the slump.[7]

Another possible source of Keynes's change of heart as regards the "state of mind of the business man" may have been his role as an investor. After Britain left the gold standard in 1931, the Bank of England was no longer bound to adjust interest rates to hold up the value of the pound sterling. As a result, long-term interest rates were no longer tethered to the short-term interest rates controlled by the Bank of England. It slowly became clear to Keynes that interest rates in the markets for long-term bonds would be determined by the psychology of those who participated in the markets. There was now a fundamental uncertainty about where interest rates would settle, and the idea of a "natural" rate of interest no longer seemed to make sense. Bit by bit, Keynes began to see that eventually the rate of interest would be set by the expectations that bond traders held about what rates would be in the future.

But if we ultimately do not know what caused Keynes to change his mind and embrace the idea that investment was driven not just by interest rates, but also by investors' expectations of the future, there is one piece of his correspondence in 1933 that provides strong circumstantial evidence: the letters between Keynes and Henderson. Not only had Henderson coauthored *Can Lloyd George Do It?* with Keynes; he was also a Cambridge-trained economist, and he had been the editor of *The Nation* after Keynes had helped take over publication of the magazine in 1923. The two were thus old friends and old allies in Liberal politics. But by 1933 Henderson had changed his mind about public-works projects as a response to the Depression, and he engaged Keynes in a spirited correspondence about the topic.

The crux of Henderson's point was that if businessmen did not believe that public-works projects would stimulate the economy, or worse, if such projects caused them to have cold feet about their own investments, the net result would not be good. In the midst of their correspondence, Henderson confirms what we know from the *Treatise on Money* and from Keynes's exchange with Pigou in the Macmillan Committee: early in 1933, Keynes refused to accept that expectations played any role in the business cycle. Writing on February 28, 1933, Henderson says to Keynes, "You often say, 'it's nonsense to talk about confidence.'"[8] And yet, by the time of Keynes's lectures at Cambridge that autumn, on what he was by then calling "the monetary theory of production," expectations and confidence suffused every aspect of his work. At the time, Keynes lectured from galley proofs of *The General Theory* that he had paid out of his own pocket to have typeset. In the autumn of 1932, the confidence of businessmen in the economy played no role in the lectures; but in the autumn of 1933, expectations of the future were important for every equation in the theory he was developing.

In particular, Keynes made expectations of the future central to the behavior of those who trade in the bond markets and also to those who borrow money to make investments in new plant and machinery. The results are now very well known. If bond traders are skittish about the future, they will demand higher returns on their investments, driving up interest rates. If investors in new capital goods lose their optimism about the future because they do not expect good profits, they will not invest. In either case, the economy is likely to get stuck at a level of output at which there is high unemployment. Thus expectations lie at the heart of his explanation of mass unemployment. They also explain why, though public works may be an essential ingredient in stimulating recovery, Keynes now believed that their effect might be less than the multiplier would suggest: Keynes openly acknowledged Henderson's argument, made three years earlier, that businessmen might get frightened by the public works and reduce their own investment.

To the extent that he talked about improving the prospects of the unemployed in *The General Theory*, aside from a short discussion of public works in the context of explaining the multiplier, Keynes did so mostly in the final chapter under the guise of what he termed the "socialisation of investment."

> The State will have to exercise a guiding influence on the propensity to consume partly through its scheme of taxation, partly by fixing the rate of interest, and partly, perhaps, in other ways. Furthermore, it seems unlikely that the influence of banking policy on the rate of interest will be sufficient by itself to determine an optimum rate of investment. I conceive, therefore, that a somewhat comprehensive socialisation of investment will prove the only means of securing an approximation to full employment.[9]

The capitalist system had one defect—that it could not ensure that the volume of investment would be sufficient to ensure full employment—but beyond that, decisions could be left in private hands. Thus Keynes did not use the phrase "socialisation of investment" to mean the nationalization of industry or a government takeover of private enterprise: on the same page he explicitly repudiated "State Socialism." He even admitted that the classical theory could explain how resources were allocated among different investment projects. All he wanted was for government to take responsibility for ensuring that the aggregate level of investment matched the level of savings that would take place at full employment. The locution "State Socialism" was chosen, no doubt, to stir up controversy by irritating his opponents, consistent with his later remark to Roy Harrod, one of the young Keynesians, that he wanted "to raise a dust: because it is only out of the controversy that will arise that what I am saying will get understood."[10]

This wording also points to the emphasis Keynes placed on investment. He admitted, in the passage just quoted, that it might be necessary to control consumption (and hence savings) through monetary and fiscal policy, but his emphasis was on ensuring an appropriate level of investment. This might involve changes in public investment, but it differed from the constant management and fine-tuning that some of his followers advocated in that it also involved stabilizing the expectations of capitalists, a much more subtle and difficult enterprise than direct government control. Of course, public-works policy and stabilizing private investment could be connected, for the "animal spirits"—the spontaneous urge to take action even when it was impossible to justify it through rational calculation—that motivated and sustained investment might be maintained at a higher and more stable level, thereby stabilizing investment, if capitalists believed that the government would, as a matter of course, speed up (or slow down) public investment as needed to maintain full employment.

The vision of how a capitalist economy operates that Keynes put forward in *The General Theory* was not the vision of his Cambridge colleagues Marshall and Pigou, for he believed that there could be no presumption that investment would be sufficient to maintain a high level of employment. But Keynes's view of policy is closer to their ideas of incremental change and limited government intervention than it was to his own vision of activist interest-rate policy in the *Treatise*. As his ideas swung back toward the traditional Cambridge theory of the trade cycle, with its emphasis on the expectations of the future, the extent of his activism moved back toward the more subtle Cambridge approach to economic policy.

Wartime Inflation and Planning for Peace

In *The General Theory,* Keynes had developed the tools he needed to diagnose the ills of capitalism, but he had not reached any settled conclusions about the precise cures that were needed, and he was open to experiment. He had written that "only experience can show" how far the state should operate on the propensity to consume or the incentive to invest.[11] Recall also his later comments, quoted above, that his book "does not offer a ready-made remedy as to how to avoid these fluctuations" and that his proposed cures "are not worked out completely" but were "subject to all sorts of special assumptions and are necessarily related to the particular conditions of the time." But this caution and pragmatism concerning policy were lost on some of his "Keynesian" followers, who, infused with the ethos of social engineering that was pervasive after the Second World War, used his theories as the basis for simple policy prescriptions much more in keeping with the magic-formula mentality that lay behind the *Treatise*. Thus although *The General Theory* is indeed his magnum opus, to understand the way Keynes viewed his ideas we need to turn to the way he developed and applied them during the Second World War and in particular to the episode that caused his young followers to believe that he agreed with them about the nuances of economic management. This was the discussion centered on yet another pamphlet that began life as a series of newspaper articles, titled *How to Pay for the War* (1940).

During the First World War, Keynes had served in the Treasury, where he had become an expert on foreign currency trading through his work in maintaining Britain's external financial position. And as we have seen, *A Tract on Monetary Reform* dealt with his concerns regarding the inflation that developed in Britain (and the rest of Europe) during and after the war. Now, as Britain entered a second world war, Keynes saw that the theoretical framework he had developed in *The General Theory* could be used to help finance the war *and* avoid inflation. The key lay in using his theory to *reduce* demand in the economy, rather than to stimulate it. Whereas the problem during the 1920s and 1930s had been persistent unemployment caused by a chronic lack of demand, Britain faced the opposite problem during the war. With the demand for munitions and supplies pulling people into work, and with the armed services drafting young men in large numbers, there was suddenly a high demand for *all* kinds of goods and services, threatening a rapid rise in prices. Keynes's pamphlet offered an elegant solution.

His proposal was to tax the incomes of those in employment to suppress the demand for ordinary consumer goods. This move would allow resources to be plowed into the war effort without causing prices elsewhere in the economy to rise precipitously. In compensation, Keynes proposed that those who were taxed be given a rebate after the war to avoid a sudden drop of demand, effectively making the tax into a form of compulsory saving.

These savings would be spent once the war was over, thereby reducing the chances of the recession that was otherwise likely to take place when military expenditure was reduced. It would also provide a kind of rough-and-ready justice by placing purchasing power in the hands of the workers who were being forced to make sacrifices during the war. The irony in this story is that the British government adopted a version of Keynes's proposal, which meant that the first use of *The General Theory* to shape British policy was not to reduce unemployment but to prevent inflation.

Keynes himself became involved in policymaking, for in August 1940 he moved into the Treasury, with no formal position and no salary, but with the freedom to engage with anyone, at whatever level. In this informal capacity he took on the role of overseeing James Meade and Richard Stone, two young economists (both of whom were later to win the Nobel Memorial Prize) who were charged with the task of producing the national income statistics needed to calculate the amount by which spending needed to be reduced to prevent inflation. The result was that the estimates of national income that formed the basis of the 1940 budget bore the marks of Keynes's influence. Not only was *The General Theory* applied; it was quantified.

However, though Keynes was involved in the details of wartime planning, his statements during the war show that he did not subscribe to what, after the war, came to be known as "Keynesian" demand management. A crucial component of postwar Keynesianism was the use of budget deficits to regulate demand: if demand needed to be increased, taxes should be cut or public spending raised, either of which would increase the budget deficit; conversely, the deficit would be reduced when demand had to be reduced. First of all, Keynes was skeptical about the use of the budget to influence consumption. Meade floated a plan to adjust the income tax collected to pay for social insurance so that it would rise during good times and fall during bad times. The idea was that this policy would slow the economy during boom times by collecting more tax and diminishing consumption; during bad times it would boost the economy by giving people more take-home pay. Keynes wrote to Meade and explained his skepticism. "I have much less confidence than you do in off-setting proposals that aim at short-period changes in consumption . . . I think it may be a tactical error to stress so much an unorthodox method, very difficult to put over, if, in addition to its unpopularity, it is not very likely to be efficacious."[12]

In addition, Keynes was *not* a supporter of budget deficits if they took the form of borrowing to finance current expenditure. During the war, unlike during the First World War, the government made plans for what would happen during peacetime, one result being the white paper *Employment Policy,* published in 1944. During the discussions that led up to this document, which outlined policies to ensure full employment, Keynes remarked at one point that "if serious unemployment does develop, deficit financing is absolutely certain to happen, and I should like to keep free to object hereafter to the more objectionable forms of it."[13]

To understand how Keynes could advocate the use of public works to stabilize the economy and at the same time object to government deficits, we need to see how he proposed to fund investment projects. Since the 1920s, Keynes had been advocating splitting the government budget into two parts: the Exchequer budget would cover current, day-to-day, expenditure, and the public-capital budget would cover the government's investment in capital goods. Indeed, he wrote the section of the Liberal Industrial Inquiry (1928) that suggested this idea. He originally considered it no more than a matter of good accounting practice, on the grounds that it was normal for a private firm to separate its capital budget from its ordinary operating budget, and that the government should do the same. The rationale, of course, was that if money was borrowed to buy a capital good that would yield a revenue stream that could be used to pay off the borrowed funds, the implications were very different from those of borrowing to finance current expenditure.

However, the motivation for this way of constructing the government accounts changed, as Keynes came to attach more importance to changes in public investment as a countercyclical device. Ever since the publication of *The General Theory,* Keynes had held that a national board of investment should be established and that this board should maintain the construction documents and the financial plans for investments that the government could undertake over several years. In contemporary language, he proposed that the government keep a set of "shovel-ready" infrastructure projects that could be implemented at any time. Having these projects ready would overcome the argument, often made in the 1920s, that public works could not be used to stabilize the economy because construction projects took so long to plan. Keynes argued that the swings in private investment that caused the trade cycle could be dampened if entrepreneurs and business managers believed that these capital expenditures could be turned on or off as required. Careful management of public capital expenditure would stabilize private expectations, and this would, in turn, diminish the swings in the output and employment. This, of course, was one way to implement the "socialisation of investment" that he had written about in *The General*

Theory. But Keynes did not see this as deficit financing, for the public-works projects involved would pay for themselves. Thus, even if the public-capital budget changed over the cycle, the Exchequer budget would not. Keynes made it clear that he did not consider the use of the public-capital budget in this way to involve deficit financing. Thus he could write, "It is important to emphasize that it is no part of the purpose of the Exchequer or the Public Capital Budget to facilitate deficit financing, as I understand this term."[14]

International Monetary Arrangements and Bretton Woods

Using the budget to regulate the level of demand in the economy was only one of the dimensions of war finance in which Keynes was involved. When he came back into the Treasury, it was as an acknowledged authority on international finance, so he inevitably became involved in discussions of external war finance: of how Britain would finance its foreign trade. The problem here was a shortage of dollars. When the war went badly in 1940, especially after the fall of France, purchases of American military equipment accelerated, and it became clear that British reserves of gold and dollars would soon be exhausted. In addition, in order to divert its own production to the war effort, British exports were curtailed, reducing the supply of dollars. This problem was partly solved by Lend-Lease, but further loans were needed, and Keynes became actively involved in the negotiations. In 1940 Keynes also started to think about what might happen after the war: the German economics minister had made proposals for a "New Order," ending the prewar economic chaos through a system of free trade and fixed exchange rates within

Europe, and Keynes was asked to come up with a counterproposal that could form the basis for a propaganda campaign. In the early months of 1941, his proposals were widely discussed in Whitehall and with Roosevelt's special assistant Harry Hopkins when he visited London.

During the remaining war years, as well as being involved in domestic issues (on top of his role in the Treasury, he became a director of the Bank of England), ranging from the national budget to arts funding, Keynes became increasingly involved in negotiations with the Americans over both financing the war and the shape of the postwar settlement. This involved a punishing schedule, for in 1937 he had suffered a heart attack, which was followed by an infection that today could be treated easily with antibiotics. For the remaining decade of his life he was plagued with heart problems, and on his many visits to the United States he had to be accompanied by his doctor. There is thus a real sense in which he was working himself to death. And negotiations with the Americans were far from easy, for there were deep divisions over the principles on which aid was being provided, not least because the American administration was constrained by Congress, and was deeply suspicious that the British were trying to maintain an empire of which they disapproved. At home, Keynes had to deal with differences between the Bank of England and the Treasury.

The dominant fact in all these negotiations was that without American support, Britain would be bankrupt. It was clearly necessary to negotiate financial support for the duration of the war. Though there were different views about the terms on which this support should be provided, both sides agreed on the necessity for this. More contentious was what would happen at the end of the war when the Lend-Lease agreement ended. Because it had converted its industry to military production and to meeting the needs of its own population, Britain had abandoned its export markets and would not have the dollars needed to pay for imports: without American support people might starve. Keynes was a brilliant negotiator who could entrance the Americans, but his bargaining position was weak.

The Keynes plan for the postwar international monetary system, first proposed in 1941, started from the observation that there was generally a shortage of international liquidity and a bias toward deflation. He proposed to solve this by setting up a Clearing Union, or international bank. This would issue bancor (bank gold), a currency that would augment the reserves available to central banks. The rules that he proposed for this international bank were designed to overcome the problem that under the traditional regime, only countries experiencing balance of payments deficits were under pressure to take action to remedy the disequilibrium: countries in surplus could just do nothing, accumulating reserves. If deficit countries were forced to cut spending while surplus countries accumulated reserves, the result would be deflation. This need not happen if the Clearing Union's rules forced surplus countries to take action, either inflating their economies or increasing the value of their currencies. Designing workable rules was difficult enough, but the problem was made even more complicated because it was entangled with Britain's desperate need for dollars. Keynes argued that, at the end of the war, in a devastated continent, Britain would not be the obvious candidate for American assistance, which meant that any support would have to come indirectly, through stabilizing the world economy. His plan for a Clearing Union would do this.

International monetary arrangements were also entangled with issues of trade policy. At the insistence of the Americans,

Article VII of the Lend-Lease agreement, signed in February 1942, committed both countries to the ending of discrimination in international trade and the reduction of tariff barriers. The British could accept this commitment (subject to some problems related to discrimination in favor of the empire), though only as a long-term goal. At the end of the war, Britain had extensive foreign-exchange controls, and much trade was centrally managed by the government (for example, there were bulk purchasing agreements for important foodstuffs). If Britain ended trade discrimination before its exports had been raised dramatically, the Bank of England would be unable to maintain sterling's convertibility.

However, while Keynes, negotiating for Britain, wanted an international monetary system that would have sufficient flexibility to be able to cope with the problems that were expected to arise after the war, the Americans were concerned about the cost to them of any scheme and about the dangers of inflation, not deflation. The American plan, put forward in 1942, was formulated by Harry Dexter White, an economist in the U.S. Treasury (who appears to have been passing classified information to the Soviet Union). It called for the establishment of two new institutions: an International Stabilization Fund and a Bank for Reconstruction. There were parallels with Keynes's plan, but the International Stabilization Fund had a much more limited role than Keynes proposed for his Clearing Union. In particular, White's fund did not have the ability to create credit through providing overdraft facilities. The burden of adjusting to payments disequilibria fell solely on debtors, something Keynes had sought to avoid.

The British and Americans started discussing each other's plans in the summer of 1942, and over the next two years entered into negotiations that led to the setting up of the International Monetary Fund (IMF) and the International Bank for Reconstruction and Development (which later became the World Bank), the two pillars of what became known, after the resort in New Hampshire where the agreement was signed on July 22, 1944, as the Bretton Woods system. Its provisions represented a compromise between the American and British plans, albeit biased in favor of the plan coming from the country that controlled the purse strings.

In the negotiations over Bretton Woods, which ran in parallel to negotiations over American financial support for Britain, Keynes played multiple roles. He was without much doubt the world's leading monetary economist, with decades of experience as a government adviser behind him. But his stature was such that in addition to being the main technical expert on the British side, he was the natural choice to be leader of the British delegation and chief negotiator. He crossed the Atlantic many times, sometimes staying for long periods. During the final round of negotiations over Bretton Woods, which effectively lasted from when the British team landed in New York on June 16, to signature of the agreement on July 22, Keynes was indisputably the central figure. Later in the year he returned to North America for three months, negotiating for American support for Britain.

Keynes as an Economic Theorist

Though Keynes's main achievement in the realm of economic policy may have been his role, with Harry Dexter White, as the architect of the Bretton Woods system, which survived till the onset of inflation in the early 1970s, it is as an economic theorist that he is best remembered. With *The General Theory,* Keynes had at last produced the work that justified his reputation as the leading monetary theorist of his generation, containing ideas that would immediately be taken up by young economists keen to participate in the revolution for which he had called. Yet, though it rapidly became one of the most-cited books in economics, it was open to several interpretations. The explanation for this lies, as we have seen, in the way Keynes reached the position described in the book. Keynes's intellectual journey had begun with the Cambridge trade-cycle theory of his teacher, Marshall, and further elaborated by two other Cambridge colleagues Pigou and Frederick Lavington. As he became embroiled in policy debates during the 1920s, he had moved away from this perspective, basing his analysis around a theory that took him closer to the approach of the Swedish economist Knut Wicksell, whose work, ironically, was also taken up by Keynes's most prominent rival in 1930, Friedrich Hayek. However, the significance of the *Treatise on Money* lies not in the details of the theory it put forward, for Keynes rapidly abandoned its fundamental equations, but in the mentality that lay behind the book—that of trying to create a magic formula that identified the cause of problems in the economy. His keen sense of what was needed in the political arena—the very opposite of the political naïveté sometimes attributed to him—had led him to neglect the complexities that had previously been at the heart of his analysis.

Keynes's achievement in *The General Theory* was twofold. One was that he had constructed a new theory, capable of being expressed in mathematical form, that explained why capitalist economies might fail to generate full employment. The reason was that full employment required that financial markets coordinate the decisions of savers and investors so that spending on capital goods was sufficient to absorb all the savings that would be generated at full employment. The relationship between saving and investment had been central to his *Treatise on Money*, published six years earlier, but in that book he had woven it into the traditional quantity theory of money. In *The General Theory*, drawing on ideas developed in debates over public-works policy in the 1920s, Keynes used saving and investment not to explain price changes but to explain output. The result was a new way of thinking about the cycle, in which output and employment were the key variables, driven by the level of investment. This achievement was summed up in a letter written to Keynes by John Maurice Clark, a leading American economist.

> It has seemed to me that what I call the "income-flow analysis," of which yours is the most noted presentation, has done something which has not been done in comparable degree since Ricardo and Marx: namely, constructed a coherent logical theoretical system or formula, having the quality of a mechanism, growing directly out of current conditions and problems which are of paramount importance and furnishing a key to working out definite answers in terms of policy.[15]

However, there was another side to the book. Though Keynes had developed what Clark called a formula (modern economists would say a model), and this was absolutely central to his arguments, he no longer sought to focus, as he had done in the *Treatise*, on a single cause of unemployment. His concept of the multiplier has more than a touch of the "magic formula" mentality about it, but it is embedded in a framework that is much less mechanical than that of the *Treatise*. The logical mechanism provided in *The General Theory* used the rate of interest, determined by supply and demand for money, to determine investment and hence output, but this stood for a much richer, more complex, analysis of the factors that determined investment. To predict how investment would respond to changes in policy or to developments in the economy it was necessary to understand the psychology of financial markets and the factors behind "animal spirits," the complex of factors that led businessmen to invest in projects that would yield returns in a future that was, in the strict sense, unknowable. Hence we have his attempt, in 1937, to sum up the essence of his differences with his predecessors by accusing the classical theory of being "one of these pretty, polite techniques which tries to deal with the present by abstracting from the fact that we know very little about the future."[16]

Economists and historians have debated which of these represents the "true" Keynes. The answer is that, for Keynes, these were two dimensions of a single argument. Thus, after presenting the essence of his book as resting on an acknowledgment that we know nothing about the future, he went on to explain that such a view led to the theory of output that Clark described as a mechanical formula. What mattered were the central ideas, and, for reasons that we will explore in the next chapter, Keynes resisted attempts to pin his theory down to a single formulation.

The same is true of his attitude to policy. *The General Theory* was, paradoxically, his most important contribution to debates over the conduct of economic policy because, in the book, he stood back from those debates to write a book addressed to his fellow economists. He had developed his ideas, over the previous decade, as much through engagements with policymakers and writing in the press as through debates with his academic colleagues, and though his knack of simplifying what he saw as the essence of the problem was still evident in *The General Theory*, he no longer sought a magic formula with which to solve a problem. Even the multiplier, a potential magic formula if ever there was one, though central to the argument, was not elevated to this status, for he was aware, more than ever, that attention had to be paid to the psychology of the markets. Hence, beyond arguing that government had a responsibility to take action to prevent mass unemployment, and making it clear that this required maintaining a high and stable level of investment, he left open the task of working out how his ideas should be put into practice. As he explained, he was far less confident about his recommendations on policy, which reflected the circumstances of the time.

As we will see, Keynes was not only comfortable with this ambiguity: it was important for him that debate not be closed off. The same was not true of his successors, however, many of whom sought to pin him down to something far more specific, with the result that they failed to do justice to one or another aspect of *The General Theory.*

5

KEYNES'S AMBIGUOUS REVOLUTION

Keynes and His Legacy

Keynes was never a humble man. To the contrary, he had great confidence in his ability and deliberately thrust himself into the center of debates about economic policy; he had great confidence in his own views (including the confidence openly to change his mind), and he enjoyed stirring up controversy. In 1914 his return to government service happened because, when he learned about the debates that were taking place over how to respond to the developing international financial crisis, he rushed to London (not even waiting for the next train, but persuading a friend to take him on a motorcycle) to put forward his own views to the Treasury. At the Versailles peace conference, he was unhappy with the constraints that came with being a government official, and resigned so as to be free to place his views before the public. During the 1920s, he repeatedly adopted the strategy of writing a paper on a contemporary economic problem, putting it before the relevant official, and then letting himself get drawn into the debate. By the time of the Second World War, he was so well known for interjecting himself into policy debates, and so well regarded, that when we was given an office in the Treasury, his job was simply "to be Keynes"; people working on different projects brought their work to him for review, and he would write and circulate memoranda on important issues relating to the economic policy during the war and postwar reconstruction.

The fact that Keynes ended up in such a position during the war was in no way to have been expected given his unorthodox history as a controversialist. After all, his best-selling book, *The Economic Consequences of the Peace* (1919), was a denunciation of the government for which he had just been working at Versailles. Revealing what he had seen as an insider will have rankled. Likewise, his forthright essay on *The Economic Consequences of Mr Churchill* might have made politicians and civil servants chary of working with him. But despite his long commitment to the Liberal Party, he was willing to point his pen at people and policies regardless of the party from which they originated. Churchill may have been a Conservative when he made the decision to return the country to the gold standard, but Keynes's *Essays in Biography,* published in 1933, contained a portrait of the Liberal leader Lloyd George, with whom Keynes had recently worked, that was very unflattering. Ultimately, those in power seemed to accept that Keynes worked first and foremost to achieve what he believed was in the best interests of Britain, which was not always the same thing as what was best for particular parties or individual politicians.

Keynes's confidence in his own ability and his willingness to stir up controversy are nowhere more evident than in *The General Theory.* He opened with a dramatic, one-page chapter, in which he argued that the "classical" theory that had dominated economics for a hundred years was but a special case of his own theory and that its assumptions did not describe the world in which we actually live. He boldly claimed that the preceding century's economic thinking was "misleading and disastrous if we attempt to apply it to the facts of experience."[1] He thus likened his own work to what Einstein had done in physics (Pigou, in reviewing the book, pointedly wrote, "Einstein actually did for Physics what Mr. Keynes believes himself to have done for Economics").[2] And then, after *The General Theory*'s publication, when the editor of Harvard's *Quarterly Journal of Economics* brought together four of the world's leading economists to review it (Frank Taussig and Wassily Leontief from Harvard, Jacob Viner from Chicago, and Dennis Robertson from Cambridge) and those reviews turned out not to be altogether flattering, Keynes argued that his critics had simply missed the point of what he was saying. Instead of replying in detail, he wrote a single article in response to all four of his critics, devoting most of it to explaining what he had tried to say in his book. He made the bold claim that he was analyzing a world in which there is uncertainty about the future that cannot be reduced to numerical probabilities, and that the "classical" theory (and by implication his four critics) ignored this. They had failed to take account of an obvious feature of reality.

None of this indicates either modesty or doubt as to whether his theory was right. It is thus tempting to conclude that to be faithful to Keynes—to be a true Keynesian—one must completely abandon the old theory and work with the theory that he laid out in *The General Theory*. That is the position of the economists who are sometimes labeled "fundamentalist Keynesians." However, to read Keynes in this way is a mistake for it is to miss out on another side of his personality.

For all the confident remarks Keynes made about his book, there is also an interesting modesty in Keynes's approach to the theory that he had built in his magnum opus. Clear evidence of this more humble attitude is found in the reply to his critics in the 1937 *Quarterly Journal of Economics*. One of the most frequently cited remarks is his very bold description of the classical theory as a "pretty, polite technique" that rests on the assumption that we know much more about the future than we do. Such boldness, which pervades the article, hardly suggests humility.[3] However, on the next page, he wrote in a much more humble tone: "I am more attached to the comparatively simple fundamental ideas which underlie my theory than to the particular forms in which I have embodied them, and I have no desire that the latter should be crystallized at the present stage of the debate." He even conceded that "substantial points" might lie behind the criticisms being leveled at his theory.[4]

Furthermore, for all his criticisms of the "classical" theory, he did not reject it entirely. In *The General Theory,* he argued that if the problem of unemployment could be solved, the free play of economic forces could be left to determine how resources would be used. His argument was as much political as economic: "individualism, if it can be purged of its defects and its abuses, is the best safeguard of personal liberty . . . and of the variety of life . . . the loss of which is the greatest of all the losses of the homogeneous or totalitarian state."[5] That this statement of support for the "classical" theory was not an aberration is shown by an even stronger remark he made in an article published in 1946 just after his death. There, he wrote:

> I find myself moved, not for the first time, to remind contemporary economists that the classical teaching embodied some permanent truths of great significance, which we are liable today to overlook because we associate them with other doctrines which we cannot now accept without much qualification. There are in these matters deep undercurrents at work, natural forces, one can call them, or even the invisible hand, which are operating

towards equilibrium. If it were not so, we could not have got on even so well as we have for many decades past.[6]

This statement is particularly important because he makes it clear that he was not making it for the first time.

This attitude, of seeing his new theory as being provisional and of limited applicability, is consistent with his reactions to economists who, immediately after *The General Theory* was published, wrote to him about their adaptations and interpretations of the theory he had presented in the book. In virtually every case, he generously encouraged their work. The best known is probably his correspondence with John Hicks, a young economist at the London School of Economics who would eventually win the Nobel Prize in 1972 for his work on economic theory. Hicks wrote to Keynes in 1937 regarding a draft of the paper that set out the model that became the centerpiece of macroeconomics until the early 1970s and the analytical framework in which a generation of economists learned their "Keynesianism." Hicks and others, such as Roy Harrod at Oxford, were working on translating *The General Theory* into algebra, creating systems of two or three equations that could be manipulated to produce the results that Keynes had derived verbally in his book. When Hicks shared his work (including the diagram that was later to be named the IS-LM model) with Keynes, the latter replied that he liked what Hicks was doing and encouraged him to continue. Keynes did demur that Hicks's specification of his model removed the possibility of including expectations, but he did not use this to imply that Hicks's work was illegitimate or unworthy of pursuing. Quite the contrary. After reading the draft of Hicks's paper, Keynes wrote to him that he "found it very interesting and really have next to nothing to say by way of criticism."[7]

Keynes's correspondence with Abba Lerner conveys the same kind of encouragement. Keynes knew Lerner, a student at the London School of Economics, from a year that Lerner had spent as a Rockefeller fellow at Cambridge in the 1930s. In correspondence between the two, Keynes gave his approval to a sophisticated reworking of the basic model of *The General Theory* in Lerner's 1936 review of the book. By the time of the Second World War, Lerner had emigrated to the United States, where he continued to develop his model of the economy as a whole. Lerner's model was sophisticated, but mechanical, and allowed him to characterize government management of the economy as a simple process akin to driving an automobile. Keynes heard this very mechanistic model expounded during one of his wartime trips to the States, and found it simplistic with regard to policymaking and the potential for using government budget deficits to spur the economy. Still, as David Colander has shown, Keynes kept open his channels of communication with Lerner and never discouraged him in his model building, per se.[8] His only qualms regarded Lerner's quantitative estimates of the effects of his model; he did not criticize Lerner's theoretical efforts.

This list of colleagues whose work he encouraged could be extended. He made similar remarks to Robert Bryce, Brian Reddaway, and Joan Robinson, correctly noting that these authors were presenting quite varied interpretations of the book.[9] Keynes's ease in encouraging others in their work shows a clear desire on his part to establish his legacy through the development and extension of his work, rather than in demanding some kind of strict adherence to the original form of his ideas. Nowhere in the voluminous correspondence after the publication of his magnum opus does he tell anyone that he or she must adhere exactly to the form of his models in *The General Theory.* Keynes even took a relaxed attitude to his claim to have effected a revolution in economic theory. Harrod, in 1937, wrote a paper in which he remarked: "Mr Keynes has not effected a revolution in fundamental economic theory but a re-adjustment and a shift of emphasis"; Keynes's response was to say that he was shortly to present a paper in Stockholm and that he would like to present Harrod's instead of his own.[10]

Another story from the last year of Keynes's life shows a different side to his attempts at cultivating his legacy. In conversation with Friedrich Hayek in 1946, Keynes responded to Hayek's concern about what certain young Keynesians were saying by claiming that he still had the ability to turn public opinion round, should inflation become a problem. As Hayek recalled,

> Later, a turn in the conversation made me ask him [Keynes] whether he was not concerned about what some of his disciples were making of his theories. After a not very complimentary remark about the persons concerned, he proceeded to reassure me by explaining that those ideas had been badly needed at the time he had launched them. He continued by indicating that I need not be alarmed; if they should ever become dangerous I could rely upon him again quickly to swing round public opinion—and he indicated by a quick movement of his hand how rapidly that would be done. But three months later he was dead.[11]

The implication is that, though he did not agree with what some young Keynesians were doing with his ideas, he was happy to let them go ahead, and would not intervene unless he had to. It seems clear that, when it came to his legacy, Keynes's real concern was not with the exact form of his theory, but rather his larger point that a capitalist economy could be unstable and that any acceptable model of the economy must be able to show this instability.

This attitude is consistent with his approach toward the emerging field of national income accounting. Keynes encouraged James Meade and Richard Stone in their work in the British Treasury on calculating national income, and he used such methods in his own work for the 1941 budget. But though some of this work, such as calculating the inflation gap and the amount of money that had to be withdrawn from circulation to prevent inflation (through taxes, compulsory saving, or other measures), could be seen as supporting a very mechanical or, as it came to be called in the 1950s, "hydraulic" Keynesianism, Keynes considered such work entirely consistent with his own work with its emphasis on uncertainty about the future.

He encouraged other economists' work even when their models ignored many of his ideas, highlighting only a few of his larger concerns. There is therefore no evidence that he was in any way proprietary about any particular formulation of the theory that he used to make his larger point that capitalism was unstable and bereft of a mechanism that would automatically ensure the return to full employment.

The Theory That Fomented a Revolution

This self-understanding fits well with the way Keynes wrote his *General Theory.* For many of his contemporaries the book was, according to more than one reviewer, "abstruse" and "mathematical."[12] Keynes, trained in mathematics, thought as a mathematician, using mathematical concepts to structure his argument: words such as "function," "curve," and "schedule" littered its pages. And yet, for the generation who came after him, the book was a puzzle, for though the algebra was there, and could be turned into simple algebraic models of the economy that could be manipulated to yield policy conclusions, Keynes did not follow this approach. His mathematics was embedded in text in which he drew conclusions that went beyond what would have followed solely from the algebra. The explanation is that Keynes was trying to use mathematical symbols in order to obtain a first approximation of insights that could not be captured fully in his mathematical formalism.

As a disciple of G. E. Moore, Keynes attached prime importance to clear thinking and to intuition. Intuition was central to the way he approached economic theorizing, for the first and fundamental stage in the construction of an argument was intuition or vision—what he called the "grey, fuzzy, woolly monster" in one's head.[13] Keynes started with a view of the overall structure of the argument he was trying to make and believed that the details came only later. The second stage was to make precise the concepts and relations involved. The progression was thus from intuition to clear thought. However, rather than progress to a formal mathematical model, Keynes essentially stopped at this point. He did construct what would now be called models, but they were rarely complete, and, unlike in modern economics, any mathematics was always inextricably linked to analysis that was expressed verbally.

Keynes's reason for using mathematics in this way was that he took the view that to construct a fully specified formal model was to attempt to be "perfectly precise," by stating exactly what was and what was not to be included in the analysis.[14] However, given that the world was vague and complex, such an approach would be inappropriate, because some important things about the economy would inevitably be left out. This way of arguing made it better to stop with the basic concepts that provided a basis for clear thinking. Thus, although Keynes used mathematics in *The General Theory*, he refused to use a mathematical model to summarize the argument as a whole, which is why modern economists often claim that the book was not mathematical.

A clue to the way Keynes used mathematics is found in lectures that he gave in the period when he was working on *The General Theory*. Notes taken by students in 1932 contain the remark, "Equations are symbolic rather than algebraic."[15] What he meant by this was that he wanted to use algebra as a framework on which to hang a more complex verbal argument: it was as if he wanted a symbol to hold the reader's attention while he talked through what it meant. He talked about this in a passage in *The General Theory*, often cited by those who criticize the use of mathematics in economics:

> It is a great fault of symbolic pseudo-mathematical methods of formalising a system of economic analysis . . . that they expressly assume strict independence between the factors involved and lose all their cogency and authority if this hypothesis is disallowed; whereas, in ordinary discourse, where we are not blindly manipulating but know all the time what we are doing and what the words mean, we can keep "at the back of our heads" the necessary reserves and qualifications and the adjustments which we shall have to make later on, in a way in which we cannot keep complicated partial differentials "at the back" of several pages of algebra which assume that they all vanish. Too large a proportion of recent "mathematical" economics are mere concoctions, as imprecise as the initial assumptions they rest on, which allow the author to lose sight of the complexities and interdependencies of the real world in a maze of pretentious and unhelpful symbols.[16]

This passage highlights the fact that Keynes attached great significance to the precise meaning of the terms involved: merely to construct a mathematical argument, relying on the conventional meaning of terms, was wholly inadequate.

The General Theory has a very clear theoretical structure. Keynes states emphatically that his main concern is to demonstrate that there is only one level of output at which the aggregate demand for goods and services will equal aggregate supply, and that this will not necessarily correspond to full employment. His method was typically to use algebraic notation to define a problem, writing down a functional relationship or breaking down a concept into its component parts, before discussing it verbally. The algebra does little more than provide the framework for a verbal discussion, and there is virtually no manipulation of the algebra to derive further results. (There are important exceptions, such as his derivation of the multiplier, but he repeatedly adopts the method of using words to develop an idea that he first stated using algebra.)

This approach might be taken as suggesting that Keynes did not attach much importance to the mathematics. However, it can also be read the other way round—as showing that Keynes's algebra, limited as it was, was central to his method of exposition. The central theoretical argument about the possibility of insufficient aggregate demand, without which neither the book nor Keynes's policy conclusions would make any sense at all, was stated mathematically, using the language of functional relationships. Arguments that Keynes chose to express mathematically, either using algebra or using notions that were readily translatable into algebra, formed the skeleton on which all his other arguments hung. This skeleton was essentially static and even mechanical, and did not by itself capture all his views, notably on uncertainty and on how decisions were made over time; but take away the chapters in which he relies heavily on algebra, removing much of his theory of aggregate demand, and there would be nothing left of *The General Theory*. He uses his algebraic skeleton as the means to animate his intuitions regarding the instability of capitalism.

The General Theory can therefore be read as a mathematical book in that Keynes consciously framed the argument in terms of abstract functions. He could have made his central argument about aggregate demand and supply more concrete, by translating abstract functions into curves that could be drawn on the page and made more concrete; but, for whatever reason, he chose not to do so. Most of the rest of the book laid the foundations for these functions, the language and argument being chosen so as to emphasize the difficulties in reducing the analysis to algebra. It was written in a style that required the reader to think as a mathematician. This could be one reason why the older generation of economists was less receptive to the book than was the younger generation, whose mathematical skills were on average much higher than those of their elders. However, it almost invited his young followers to develop the theory in ways that he had not done.

These dimensions of Keynes's work come together to help explain why it could be read in so many different ways after his death (and even before). Though he used mathematics, some of the most important ideas were not captured in the mathematics itself. He wrote of causing a revolution in economic theory, but his revolution lay in his efforts to articulate clearly a general conception of how a capitalist economy worked, not in the mathematical details of his theory. He proposed a theory, yet encouraged his followers to develop it in different ways that were not necessarily compatible with each other. He loved to shock and to be controversial; so some of his remarks suggested, to later economists who did not know their author, views that bore little relation to ones he actually held. The way was open for multiple interpretations of Keynesian economics.

The most widespread approach became the one that Hicks and Harrod had helped to pioneer, and which Keynes encouraged: take Keynes's mathematics and turn it into a simple, two- or three-equation model of output, employment, and the rate of interest (such as the so-called IS-LM model). Such models could be manipulated to explain how Keynesian theory differed from that of his "classical" predecessors and they could then be developed in many different ways, drawing on the latest ideas about theories of households, firms, and markets. Though this modeling strategy proved immensely useful in tackling new problems, it caused serious problems for the interpretation of Keynesian economics: whereas Keynes had assumed that there were important group effects in economic behavior, the theories that later economists used to try to develop his work almost all depended on an assumption of individualist behavior that did not take account of how people might be influenced by what others were doing and thinking. Keynes had not approached theorizing in this way, choosing instead to base his theory on generalizations derived from behavior he had observed from his vantage point in the City. The result was that because most economists were trying to capture his ideas within an individualistic framework that was very different from his own, seeking to construct mathematical models of factors that Keynes had not modeled formally, there was much scope for interpreting his ideas not only in different ways, but sometimes in incompatible ways. The result was a series of debates and arguments over which interpretation represented the true

Keynesian theory, and whether different models produced conclusions that were consistent with those Keynes had reached.

Others complained that these translations of Keynesian economics, through focusing solely on his algebra, neglected the most important parts of his theory. The algebra described a static model, whereas many of his intuitions and arguments related to dynamic factors—for instance, the formation of expectations and how people responded to change. The central issue became to what extent the use of mathematics precluded the kind of verbal analysis within which Keynes had always embedded his algebra. The true Keynes, some argued, was the theorist who believed that it was impossible to know what would happen in the future, and for whom investment was driven less by rational calculation than by a spontaneous urge to do something rather than nothing, by what he called "animal spirits." If the mathematical specification of his argument meant that these factors could no longer be considered, then a mathematical model could not be a faithful representation of his ideas. Such "fundamentalist" Keynesians could find ample support in *The General Theory* and in Keynes's 1937 defense of the book, some of them denouncing the mathematical modelers as "bastard" Keynesians who were not true to Keynes's legacy.

Add to this the fact that *The General Theory* was what its title suggested—a book on economic *theory,* not a book on policy—and the possibility for confusion was even greater; for many economists believed that the importance of Keynes's theory lay in its policy implications, not in its theoretical intuitions. Alongside those trying to identify the innovations that defined the Keynesian revolution in economic theory, others saw the Keynesian revolution primarily in terms of policies to manage the level of aggregate demand. Because Keynes had written *The General*

Theory as a book about the theory of employment, not as a systematic treatise on controlling the economy, there was scope for different interpretations of this revolution, too.

In one sense, this is precisely what Keynes wanted—that subsequent generations would take his ideas and run with them in many different directions, while preserving his basic ideas. Indeed, by 1937 he was himself already looking to move on from *The General Theory,* as he explained in a letter to his young colleague Joan Robinson. Not only did he encourage her to proceed with her own book, which he described as "practically following my *General Theory,*" but he added, "I am gradually getting myself into an outside position towards the book, and am feeling my way to new lines of exposition."[17] For thirty years or more, economists accepted his idea that there could be involuntary unemployment, caused by a deficiency in the level of aggregate demand, and though they had different views on how this could be addressed, they continued to work out policies to remedy this defect in capitalism. In accepting that there could be a shortage of aggregate demand they were following Keynes. However, in their heated, almost theological debates, over what was the true Keynesian theory, many economists adopted an attitude that was radically different from Keynes's own openness to experimentation and adaptation within a basic algebraic framework.

This attitude, of trying to find the single, true Keynesian theory, reflected a change in the way economists conceived their subject. After the Second World War, economists increasingly began equating economic theory with models that were sufficiently precise that they could be expressed using exact mathematics, and confining their conclusions to results that could be shown to follow from those models. Finding Keynes's theory became trying to work out Keynes's "model," which led to fundamental difficulties because Keynes did not work with a model in the same way that succeeding generations of economists did. Whereas he had seen his mathematical functions and formulas as a way to organize his fundamental insights in a coherent way, and then used them to animate different stories about how the economy worked, the most influential economists after the Second World War sought fully specified models that could be used to generate clear predictions; if possible, ones that could be tested against statistical data. Increasingly, their method left much less room for factors that could be brought in later in the verbal development of their models.

Keynes's Revolutionary Policy

There was a parallel ambiguity in the revolution Keynes fomented in economic policy. Though he is widely seen as one of the architects of the welfare state, having designed the full-employment policies without which the welfare state could not function, his own views on policy were very different. He saw the goal of government policy as being to overcome "the dark forces of time and ignorance."[18] Keynes believed that the long-term expectations of investors, which are as much the product of "animal spirits" as of rational calculation, are based on conventions and beliefs that may change at a moment's notice, and with them investment. There was a role for the state in Keynes's vision, but he was ineluctably committed to the idea that private investment was the key to prosperity. Keynes recognized that there were times when regulating consumption was needed (notably in wartime, when it was clear that consumption had to be reduced to release resources for the war effort), and he was quite willing to make his point about the occasional need for more government spending by using the example of burying banknotes in the ground and digging them up again; but his main focus, both in *The General Theory* and before, was on stabilizing investment. Even in the depths of the Great Depression, when many factories were unused and the construction of new plant and equipment was not an obvious response to the ongoing devastation, he focused on measures to increase investment.

The importance Keynes attached to investment is made clear in a report Keynes wrote for the Dutch company Philips in 1930. He had been employed for several years writing economic reports for Philips, and as the world fell into depression, factories fell idle. When Keynes talked in his report about the need for new investment, his contact at Philips asked him whether new investment would not simply exacerbate the problem of excess capacity. Keynes replied that he did not mean investment in manufacturing, but investment in new buildings, transport, and public utilities. There was a need to modernize plant in manufacturing industry, but the scale of the investment required was smaller than what was needed for these other purposes. The point is that even under the circumstances of the unfolding depression, Keynes believed there were opportunities for productive investment, and he sought means to encourage it, notably through keeping long-term interest rates low.

This emphasis on investment continued in *The General Theory*. When Keynes came to speculate on the social philosophy toward which his theory might lead, he explored the consequences, not of a high level of employment (one could imagine others speculating on the possibilities this would open up for social insurance, welfare provision, or redistribution) but of flooding the world with capital, to the point where it was no longer scarce. The prospect of what he called "the euthanasia of the rentier" may seem naïve in failing to see the extent to which human wants would increase, but it nonetheless indicates the centrality of investment to his view of the world.[19]

The centrality of investment to both Keynes's diagnosis of the problems with capitalism and the solution to these problems explains how he could argue for measures to combat depression while supporting the idea that the government budget should be balanced. As was explained in Chapter 4, not only was he skeptical about whether proposals to stabilize the economy through changes in social-security contributions would work, but he found certain forms of debt-financed expenditure "objectionable." Debt should be used to fund investment, not spending on consumption. This was why be proposed setting up a capital budget, separate from the ordinary budget. The former could be used to stabilize the economy, allowing debt that resulted in the creation of productive assets, without creating the temptation to use borrowing to fund current spending.

There was also his famous argument for the "socialisation of investment" in the concluding chapter of *The General Theory.* Though the phrase may have been chosen deliberately to be provocative, he did not mean state control of investment as would take place in a centrally planned economy. Rather he meant, as was explained in Chapter 4, a system where the state took responsibility for the *volume* of investment, seeking to keep it from fluctuating or getting stuck at a dangerously low level. One key was monetary policy, and low long-term interest rates, but he recognized that if expectations were depressed, more might be required than low interest rates. If it were known that the state would maintain aggregate investment, resorting to debt-financed public investment where it was required, this might be enough to reassure private investors, thereby achieving stability without the need to incur deficits.

But this is a long way from the welfare state. Keynes was familiar with the idea of the welfare state, and, as noted in Chapter 2, during the Second World War he worked with William Beveridge on his influential government policy document, *Social Security and Allied Services* (1942); but his role was limited. It was Beveridge, not Keynes, whose vision lay behind the proposals—indeed, Beveridge had not been enthusiastic about *The General Theory* when it was published. Skeptical about the very low unemployment targets that Beveridge was proposing, Keynes's principle role was to help Beveridge pare down his proposals so that they would be financially affordable, yet another instance of his concern with sound fiscal policy. Clearly, full employment was a key element in the welfare state, for otherwise it would be impossible to afford a comprehensive system of social security; but this set of circumstances does not make Keynes its architect. His own ideas on the role of policy were very different indeed.

The Artist and His Theory

In some senses the creation of a Keynesianism that departed from Keynes's own ideas is not remarkable. Keynes was most interested in developing a diagnostic toolkit and in using that toolkit to diagnose the problems facing contemporary capitalism, so what he most wanted was good tools for the task at hand. His only insistence was that economists and politicians should no longer deny that the patient could be ill, even gravely ill. The tools did not matter so long as there was no pretense that the patient could heal himself. However, there is more to Keynes's attitude than his insistence that other practitioners share his vision of capitalism as fragile, and sometimes in need of help. Over the previous thirteen years, he had developed several theories of his own and had seen many of these come to naught. Having been governed by a "magic formula mentality" while working on the *Treatise,* he had ended up with something unwieldy and mechanistic that had not worked. Now he could appreciate a more flexible way of understanding economic phenomena: possibly, even in the joy of his hard-won theoretical triumph in *The General Theory,* he realized that in the long run, all theories must die.

Keynes's view of his *General Theory* was that of an artist who has reached a point of self-understanding that allowed him to see his own creative work in a longer historical perspective. However, this way of seeing Keynes is not simply a metaphor inspired by his membership in Bloomsbury, for it is wrong to see him as an economist who happened to live among artists. He was an integral part of Bloomsbury, and his work must be seen as an expression of his own artistic beliefs. His attitude of seeing his artistic success as providing a foundation on which others would build was more than a pragmatic realization of the nature of artistic achievement: it was also part of a complicated ethical stance that eschewed material gain as the highest end of life, while simultaneously denying the authority of tradition. Rather than adopt the strategy of his Cambridge mentor, Moore, who built his argument for the primacy of art on intuitions about what constitutes the good life, Keynes was drawn to the ideas of his Bloomsbury friend, the art critic Roger Fry. Alongside the need for humans to satisfy their material needs for food, shelter, and reproduction, the sphere of existence he referred to as their "actual lives" stood the "imaginative life," defined by the "arts, literature and disinterested inquiry."[20] As society became richer, art would become increasingly important. According to Fry,

> the imaginative life comes in the course of time to represent more or less what mankind finds to be the most complete expression of its own nature, the freest use of its innate capacities, the actual life may be explained and justified by its approximation here and there, however partially and inadequately, of that freer and fuller life.[21]

An illustration of Keynes's attitude is given by the presidential address he delivered to the annual reunion of the Apostles in 1921. What had united the Apostles of Keynes's own generation were their commitments, learned from G. E. Moore, to what they saw as absolute truth and to the search for friendship and beauty. The ideal career for many of Keynes's cohort of Apostles would have been to become an artist, creating beauty and living in a community of other artists with whom one had close bonds of friendship. But what should one do if one did not have the talent to become an artist? In his address, Keynes seems to suggest that the best option for those who lack artistic talent may be to use their talents to pursue a career in finance or business. Following the seventeenth century poet and playwright Ben Jonson, however, Keynes argued that the true reward of such activity lay not in wealth itself so much as in the way it was achieved, quoting Jonson's *Volpone* (Act 1, Scene 1) to make his point:

> Yet I glory
> More in the cunning purchase of my wealth
> Than in the glad possession.

Though this raises the question of why he chose finance and business rather than any other career as the best alternative for those who lacked artistic talent, what is significant here is that even as an established economist, and after the enormous success of *The Economic Consequences of the Peace,* Keynes was still contemplating how to fulfill his own artistic ambitions. It is significant that when he realized that the *Treatise on Money* was not the work he had hoped it would be, he chose to describe it as an "artistic failure."

The desire of this practical, applied economist, whose aim was to diagnose remedies for capitalism's ills, for a major achievement in economic theory was very much a reflection of the values of Bloomsbury, whose members saw the creation of art as one of the highest human activities. Similarly, his willingness to take the long view of his work reflected Bloomsbury's expectation that others would follow down their path and build upon their creative successes, taking them in new directions, just as the Post-Impressionists had built upon the work of the Impressionists. In 1921, when he addressed the Apostles, Keynes had wondered what a person who did not possess any artistic talent was to do in order to lead a meaningful life; perhaps in 1936, in the moment of his own creative success, he was coming to understand his work in the same way that an artist might understand his.

And, of course, Bloomsbury was notorious for its refusal to accept the authority of tradition. In their painting, their novels, and their polemics, they reacted against the traditional morality of the Victorian age into which they had been born. In this, Keynes was also a full member of Bloomsbury. One of the first high-profile successes of the original members of the group was Lytton Strachey's *Eminent Victorians,* which consisted of four biographical sketches, meant to show the hypocrisy of Victorian values. Keynes used the same technique of devastating biographical sketches in the portraits he wrote of the world leaders at Versailles in his *Economic Consequences of the Peace,* written shortly after Strachey's book appeared. His denunciations of *The Economic Consequences of Mr Churchill* and of "classical" economics in *The General Theory* were in the same vein. It was also in this vein that, in correspondence, he referred to the efforts of two of his older Cambridge colleagues to hold on to their old theories in the face of their newfound support for public-works projects as "a sort of Society for the Preservation of Ancient Monuments."[22]

This aversion to tradition was not simply a rhetorical device for attacking those with whom members of the Bloomsbury group disagreed. It also applied to their own work, for when discussing things among themselves, they never considered a subject closed. They did not want their own ideas to become an orthodoxy. This wish was clearly expressed by Fry, who wrote, in words that could have been used by Keynes, "I have always looked on my system with a certain suspicion. I have recognised that if it ever formed too solid a crust it might stop the inlets of fresh experience."[23]

Bloomsbury's stance against the authority of tradition caused some awkwardness for them, of course, when others attacked their own positions. For who were they to replace the authority of the Victorians with an authority they had created for themselves? The way out of this dilemma that they often took was simply not to respond to their critics. Their silence was often taken as arrogance, when it was actually meant as a way to allow others to express their opinions and develop their own ideas. Keynes could be withering in his response to his critics, but he sometimes remained silent. He did respond to critics of *The General Theory,* though not in the detail to which they might have felt entitled. But the fullest expression of the artistic sensibility that he cultivated as a member of Bloomsbury was his response to the young economic theorists who first worked to expand and elaborate his ideas in the year or two after he had published the book. Having finally accomplished his own "artistic" success, he now had the magnanimity to respond generously and to encourage their experiments.

Keynes's Revolution

Keynes caused a revolution, but the nature of his revolution has been disputed, and the controversy over what it comprised shows no sign of abating. This is no accident, for there are many features of his work that have caused his *General Theory* to be understood in different ways. He was trained as a mathematician and used the language of mathematics in composing the book; and yet he believed that the math was merely a way of capturing his basic intuitions, and some of his most important points were never captured in the equations. When the economics profession turned to a new kind of formal mathematical modeling after the Second World War, however, much of what was most important to him about his work, such as his belief that capitalism could be unstable and was not always a self-correcting mechanism, was lost in the effort to formalize his theories.

His generosity to his younger colleagues did not help. Some of the formalizations of his work that ultimately undercut his most basic intuitions were those first pioneered by people he encouraged, such as Hicks and Lerner. They did not abandon Keynesianism, but in the hands of others, their models led in that direction. Keynes had encouraged his younger colleagues because he believed that his ideas should be developed in new forms. Creative adaptation and new variations on one's work are what one should expect if one's work is successful. To have produced work so good that others extended and elaborated it as an expression of their own imaginative lives was the thing that Keynes valued above all else, save perhaps friendship.

However, there is yet another reason for the ambiguity of Keynes's legacy. During the time that Keynes was finishing the *Treatise on Money* and beginning *The General Theory,* he was a strong proponent of large-scale public-works projects to stimulate the economy out of depression. His support for public works is clearest in *Can Lloyd George Do It?* and *The Means to Prosperity.* As he continued to work on *The General Theory,* however, and fully took on board the importance of uncertainty and expectations, he developed a more cautious approach to public works; he came to see the validity of the arguments of his critics (some of whom, such as Henderson, had also once been his allies) that large-scale public works depended for their success upon the confidence of private investors. Accordingly, he developed an argument for their use that was more nuanced and acknowledged that the task at hand was more the subtle problem of the "socialisation of investment" (in the sense described in Chapter 4) than it was of government control of the economy through fiscal policy. Although Keynes had declared in his last years that he was not advocating government budget deficits, many people took his theories as making the case for deficit-financed stabilization policy. This complicated legacy for his policies has led to serious ambiguity. Critics and supporters of his policies alike drew caricatures of his ideas (indeed, the modern welfare state, reliant on levels of unemployment that were lower than he believed possible, was arguably based on one such caricature). Few understood the caution that followed the full development of his *General Theory,* or the nuance involved in his policy stances. The Keynesian revolution may have been far-reaching, but it was ambiguous.

6

PERPETUAL REVOLUTION

After the Crisis

In 2008–09 the world's financial system came close to collapse, raising the prospect of an uncontrollable fall into depression: it looked as though it might be 1929 all over again. The policies that had supported "the great moderation" of the previous two decades were suddenly irrelevant: the world needed new policies urgently, and it turned to Keynes, or rather to the economist it believed was Keynes. Low interest rates and fiscal stimulus were policies straight out of the Keynesian lexicon—and they worked. Keynes, the economist whose theories had apparently been discredited by the experiences of the 1970s and 1980s and by dramatic advances in macroeconomic theory, was vindicated. Even well-known conservatives like Richard Posner could see that markets had failed and that action needed to be taken to prevent further collapse.

The crisis was significant because it raised a wide range of questions concerning the way the financial system was organized and, ultimately, about the type of capitalism that had come to dominate the world economy. The immediate cause of the crisis was the meltdown of much of the banking system, caused by the cocktail of subprime mortgages, credit default swaps, collateralized debt obligations, and other financial instruments held by the banks. The drive to mortgage securitization that created this situation arose in part because of the fragmented nature of the U.S. banking system, with its thousands of banks, which was the result of regulations dating back to the nineteenth century. Furthermore some of the key institutions in the financial sector, Fannie Mae and Freddy Mac, whose collapse was a key element in the crisis, were created by government. However, though important features of the system were the result of government intervention to control the power of banks and to increase the flow of affordable mortgages, a major element in the crisis, albeit not the whole story, was the relaxation of regulations that had taken place since the mid-1970s. The "light touch" regulatory system that had emerged allowed the banks to mix these toxic assets together in their portfolios and also meant that there was no readily available means for investors or regulators to know what toxic assets each bank held. Thus, once the system started to collapse, it was virtually impossible to tell whether many banks simply faced liquidity problems or whether they had become insolvent. The deregulation of the banking system had left the banks in serious trouble, and had also obscured just how badly in trouble they were.

Another result of the deregulation of the system was that commercial banking, which had traditionally made profits through the margin between borrowing and lending, had become entangled with investment banking, reliant on hefty fees and, to put it bluntly, gambling for its profits. But the problems were not confined to the banks, for the regulatory changes that had affected banking were part of a much broader transformation of financial markets. This had started with the establishment of the Chicago Board Options Exchange on April 26, 1973,[1] which had created a market in stock options and begun the process whereby derivatives trading began to dominate the entire financial sector. Deregulation had eliminated the rules that separated different types of financial institutions and also lay behind the changing regime of monetary policy; for in a world where banks could create new assets and move funds around the world faster than the traditional means of monetary control could keep up with them, a new modus operandi for monetary policy had inevitably become necessary. Financial liberalization also underwrote enormous changes in the real economy, with a range of financial instruments from junk bonds to private equity being used to restructure manufacturing industries.

This process of financial liberalization was not an isolated phenomenon, but was part of a much broader move toward liberalizing markets aimed at enabling not just capital but labor and goods to move more freely between different parts of the world. Though it has affected all countries, this system-wide policy of liberalization has been most evident, and arguably most controversial, in Third World countries, where the policies involved have been described as the "Washington Consensus"—the label for a package of measures that has often been imposed on countries seeking financial assistance from the International Monetary Fund or the World Bank, often as part of "structural adjustment programs." Many countries, from Latin America in the 1980s to East Asia in the late 1990s, were required not just to reform their monetary and financial systems, or even to tackle government finance, but also to privatize government-owned businesses, to dismantle trade barriers, and to allow foreign firms to enter their domestic markets. Free-market capitalism, of which a deregulated financial system was an integral part, was seen as the route toward prosperity for *all* economies. Joseph Stiglitz, the controversial chief economist at the World Bank at the time of the East Asian financial crisis in 1998, has argued that this crisis and others in Third World countries presaged the bigger crisis of 2008–09. These outwardly different crises were the result of the same free-market ideology, and in the same way he had argued against the International Monetary Fund's recommendations of tight monetary policy in 1998 on the grounds that it would exacerbate the crisis through raising the prospect of bankruptcy, he has been critical of restrictive policies in the current crisis.

The ideology of market liberalization was given an enormous boost by the collapse of Communism in the Soviet Union and Eastern Europe in 1989–1991. This collapse was widely taken to have vindicated those economists who had claimed that centrally planned economies could not work—that the problems with the Soviet system were inherent in any nonmarket economy and were not the result of factors specific to the Soviet Union (such as an economic system forged against the background of civil war, political repression, and Stalin's interpretation of Marxism-Leninism). Hostility to Communism was translated into suspicion of anything that might interfere with the operation of an unregulated capitalism. As a result, the former Communist countries generally sought to emulate not the welfare capitalisms of Western Europe, with their extensive regulatory regimes, but the free-market capitalism advocated by Milton Friedman and Friedrich Hayek. However, as Alan Greenspan, onetime follower of libertarian philosopher Ayn Rand, famously confessed when testifying before Congress, on October 23, 2008, after the recent financial crisis it became clear to many people that this free-market ideology was no longer working.

By the beginning of 2010, the attention of free marketers had shifted away from reforming the financial system to the problem of government debt. Despite the role that fiscal stimulus had played in averting disaster in 2009, an effort was now made to focus instead on the long-term accumulation of debt that had been occurring for several decades, and rose sharply after the banks were bailed out and Keynesian fiscal stimuli were introduced. In the United States, the ratio of government debt to national income rose from 64 percent in 2007 to 83 percent in 2009, and threatened to rise even further if measures were not taken to reduce the government's annual deficit. Some other countries saw even more rapid increases in their debt as the recession hit their tax revenues and compounded the deficits created by the emergency spending on fiscal stimulus. Even if desperate measures had been needed to avert a second Great Depression (and by 2010 dissenting voices had begun to argue that the fiscal stimulus of 2008–09 had been an overreaction), it was becoming clear that government deficits would eventually need to be brought under control. Their size meant that this could not be done through small adjustments in taxes or government spending. Furthermore, the increased fluidity of world financial markets meant that countries could not wait for economic growth and inflation to solve the problem (this was how debt-income ratios had been reduced after the Second World War). The reason the problem could not be solved as it had been in the past was that bond market traders were frightened that inflation might arise when the economy started to grow, and that this would cause interest rates to rise and choke off investment. In order to avoid inflation, they argued that it was necessary to cut government spending.

The crisis, though it had started in the banking sector, thus raised deeper questions that extended beyond reform of the financial system, beyond the question of what type of capitalism should be created, to the type of society that was to be created. This was clearly expressed by the newly elected British prime minister, David Cameron, when he warned of the need for cuts in public spending that would change the shape of British society. What had started as an economic crisis, centered on a deregulated financial world that had until then been invisible to most people, had ended up raising questions that were clearly political in that they involved choices about what the entire social welfare system should look like. When people had been confronted with the seriousness of the financial crisis when Lehman Brothers collapsed in 2008, it had not been obvious to anyone that the outcome of the efforts to ameliorate the effects of the crisis would be to call into question the affordability of the welfare state.

On most other occasions when radical economic change has been contemplated, there has seemed to be a clear direction in which to move. For example, there had been no doubt, in Russia in 1990, that the socialist economic system needed to be dismantled and replaced by capitalism (there was, of course, much debate about how this should be achieved, though little about the eventual goal). But in 2009–10 the problem was that it was not possible to move from a failed free-market capitalism to an even more thoroughly discredited socialism. There was thus a need to work out an alternative. This dilemma was particularly acute for the left, which in more "normal" times should have benefited from a crisis in laissez-faire ideology. This was put eloquently by British historian Tony Judt:

> Why do we experience such difficulty in even imagining a different sort of society? Why is it beyond us to conceive a different set of arrangements to our common advantage? Are we doomed

> indefinitely to lurch between a dysfunctional "free market" and the much-advertised horrors of "socialism"? Our difficulty is discursive: we simply do not know how to talk about these things any more.[2]

To many, it seemed obvious that a better society should be "greener" and more sustainable, and to others that it should be fairer, reversing the seemingly inexorable rise in inequality that, over the previous three decades, had undone the progress toward greater equality made in the three decades immediately after the Second World War. However, on their own, such aspirations were not enough to show either how a new society should be organized or what measures needed to be taken to create it.

It became clear during the crisis that academic economics, at least as it then was, could not say what this new society should look like. Economists could offer considerable understanding of small parts of the system, such as how incentives might affect the way managers behaved, but no understanding of how these small parts fitted together. One problem, of course, was that the mainstream of the profession had completely failed to see that a crisis was likely, or even inevitable, because they had not been fully aware of what was going on in the financial sector and why it might be important; a comparatively small number of economists, of whom Nouriel Roubini probably gave the most detailed forecast of what was in store, had publicly predicted the crisis, but it remained the case that the dominant macroeconomic models *had* fostered a blindness toward the problems that proved to be crucial.

However, the larger problem for economists was that the crisis had a moral dimension. Though the supporters of free-market capitalism had been able to call upon economic theory before the crisis to provide arguments that free, competitive markets were efficient, and that government intervention would often make markets perform badly, the case for free-market capitalism was, nonetheless, fundamentally a moral one that did not depend on economic theory. The moral argument was that people were entitled to what they could get in the free market, even if this was a multimillion-dollar reward for doing little or no real work; likewise, it was taken as a moral argument that taxes were an intrusion on private property. It might be recognized that taxes were necessary, for certain public services had to be financed (and because of their belief in the welfare state most continental Europeans, at least in the "old" Europe, were willing to tolerate higher levels of taxation than were Americans), but they were still seen as an intrusion on private property. Thus, when the problems with national debt levels came to the fore in 2010 as government deficits ballooned, the common presumption was that, even though the cause was as much falling taxation brought about by the recession as it was the stimulus packages that had been instituted, the remedy was assumed to involve cuts in public spending, not rises in taxation, for this would not be morally acceptable. But for better or worse, the economics profession had long ago given up on trying to examine moral questions when it declared itself a "value-free" science in the mid-twentieth century.

The crisis of capitalism that emerged in 2008–09 was thus entangled with two sets of moral, political, and ideological beliefs. On the one hand, there was the set of free-market beliefs which Alan Greenspan admitted were no longer working as an economic argument, but which still animated many people's beliefs about the legitimacy of the state. On the other hand, there was the ideology that underlay the post–Second World

War settlement, including the recovery of Europe from the political turmoil of the 1920s and 1930s, and is best labeled social democracy. This second set of beliefs was also nicely captured by the term used by German liberals after 1945 to describe their new economic regime: the social market economy. The market—capitalism—was central, but it was recognized (very clearly in Germany after the experience of the Nazi period) that it needed to be controlled. A generous welfare state, controlled by a democratically elected, representative government, was considered as important to economic success as were free markets. The welfare state was, moreover, necessary to ensure freedom, for it was part of the package that could prevent a repetition of what had happened before the war. The social-market economy was a German phenomenon, but despite the differences, elements of this social-democratic ideology were prominent in most of the developed world. Even in the United States, though businessmen might rail against Roosevelt and denounce the New Deal, capitalism had evolved after the Second World War as an institution in which markets, democracy, and welfare provision seemed sustainable. Now, following the financial crisis of 2008–09 and the fiscal crisis of 2010, the two ideologies were in a standoff. Capitalism had been revealed to not work well, but social democracy was argued to be unsustainable.

The Moral Foundations of Capitalism

Paradoxically, the challenge of developing a new moral foundation for capitalism brings us back to Keynes, just as squarely as did the need for policies to prevent another Great Depression. It is wrong to conclude that because the urgent problem is now seen to be deficit reduction, calling into question the affordability of the welfare state, Keynes is an irrelevance. On the contrary, he addresses the current situation as much as that of the crisis years of 2008–09; but we now need a different Keynes.

Keynes was an economist—he was even an economist with an advanced training in mathematics—but, unlike most modern economists, he was also a moral philosopher who developed a vision of capitalism that could potentially be of value today. His vision was of a capitalism that was immensely fragile, something that resonates after the experience of 2008–09 and the various financial crises, including the 1987 stock market crash, the Asian financial crisis of 1997, and the dot-com bubble of 2001. He was a classical liberal in his politics, being as attached to individual freedom as the most ardent libertarian, who throughout his life repudiated socialism and chose to remain in the doomed Liberal Party rather than join the emerging Labour Party. Yet he remained firmly on the left, seeking to use the resources of the state to create a better society. And in an age that has become suspicious of, and even cynical about, easy solutions, his skeptical attitude to simple formulas, and his pragmatic openness to a range of solutions, give his work a contemporary tone.

The resonance of Keynes's ideas with today's concerns should not be a surprise. When we think of Keynes, our thoughts turn first to the Great Depression; but the entire period from 1914 to 1945 was one of turmoil, in which economists and policymakers had to confront not only the problem of unemployment but also violent business cycles, hyperinflation, financial crises, deflation, and the breakdown of world trade. It is not just the generation that lived through the 1970s that learned about the importance of inflationary expectations; economists in the 1920s, on whose work Keynes built, were well aware of the problem.

It is also no coincidence that Keynes tackled explicitly the problem of capitalism's legitimacy, for this was the period when capitalism was being questioned more strongly than at any other period in history. The field of "comparative economic systems," in which students compared capitalism and socialism, may not have emerged until the 1960s, at the height of the Cold War, but for Europeans of Keynes's generation there was even more reason to believe that capitalism might not survive and that it should not be taken for granted. The task of reform was much more urgent than it was when, as in the 1950s and 1960s, capitalism appeared to be working well: for most of the period after the Second World War, the Soviet Union might have posed a serious military threat, but it was not winning the ideological war.

Thus Keynes offers us a vision of capitalism in which economic and moral analysis are intertwined. He saw the importance of liberty, in markets as much as in politics, but he had no illusions that markets always worked perfectly. To the contrary, capitalism was a highly imperfect system that needed government intervention if it was to work properly. Equally, though liberty was a fundamental value, Keynes did not see competition as a moral ideal: to the contrary, it was morally questionable but, at the same time, essential. Though he did not deny the legitimacy of private incomes, acquired through markets, he would not condemn state intervention (even taxation) as immoral in itself.

For Keynes, as we explained in Chapter 3, the real problem was that capitalism had to be materially very successful to maintain its legitimacy; but its tendency to veer into instability and prolonged periods of mass unemployment made legitimacy difficult to sustain. The interwar period, of unprecedented economic instability, was thus a time when capitalism was called into question as never before. Keynes did not like the greed that he believed animated many capitalists, but he believed that it was the system that provided more potential for personal liberty and material well-being than any other. The problem, then, was how to make capitalism more stable so that it could deliver these other benefits.

Keynes was not naïve about this problem. He understood that at its heart, capitalism required that the animal spirits—the spontaneous optimism—of entrepreneurs be high to attain the success he believed that it needed to establish its legitimacy. He never argued that the state could run capitalism better than capitalists could. What he did believe was that low interest rates and a carefully planned system of public-works projects might stabilize private investment. He recognized that such a policy could backfire if it caused anxiety among investors, but this all the more clearly made the problem of sustaining capitalism a moral problem, rather than an engineering one. There was a role for the state in stabilizing animal spirits, but exactly how to achieve this end remained to be worked out. Keynes called neither for the state to do what entrepreneurs could better do themselves, nor for the state to fine-tune the economy.

The Role of the State

The argument for laissez-faire—for leaving business to get on with making money—rests on the assumption that, in furthering their own interests, businessmen will take actions that benefit society. Capitalists will make profits, but in doing so they will create jobs and produce goods that people want to buy. And yet, even before the Great Depression struck, Keynes was having doubts about this view. He wrote, "the great captain of industry, the master-individualist, who serves us in serving himself, just as any artist does . . . is becoming a tarnished idol. We grow more doubtful whether it is he who will lead us into paradise by the hand."[3] Similarly, after the 2008 crisis, though we might be skeptical about the state we also have good reasons to doubt that the world can be left to free enterprise. In the essay from which this quotation is taken, *The End of Laissez-Faire* (1926), Keynes sought principles for deciding the role of the state in a world in which we have confidence neither in unregulated capitalism nor in socialism.

His starting point was the claim that the division between what he called the agenda and the non-agenda of the state could not be determined on abstract grounds. The choice between individualism and state socialism was a false one, because it overlooked the details of how institutions, intermediate in size between the individual and the state, worked. Socialists were, Keynes argued, wrong to nationalize industry in order to produce goods more efficiently than they were produced by private enterprise. Instead, the state should do things that private enterprise could not do.

> The most important *Agenda* of the State relate not to those activities which private individuals are already fulfilling, but to those functions which fall outside the sphere of the individual, to those decisions which are made by *no one* if the state does not make them. The important thing for government is not to do things which individuals are doing already, and to do them a little better or a little worse; but to do those things which at present are not done at all.[4]

His main example of something that could be done only by the state was mitigating the effects of risk, uncertainty, and ignorance, which caused business to become a lottery, creating great disparities of wealth. The state should both control money and credit, and disseminate information so as to reduce uncertainty. His second example went further: the control of savings and investment. This would need to cover deciding both how much should be saved and invested, and how much investment should flow abroad and how much remain at home.

Both of Keynes's last two books of economic theory, *A Treatise on Money* and *The General Theory,* were influenced by his insights in *The End of Laissez-Faire.* In the *Treatise,* he grappled at length, and without success, with the question of how to coordinate the separate decisions of savers and investors through a better interest-rate policy. In fact, this unsuccessful effort defined the nature of his "artistic failure." But once he had discovered a mechanism to explain how output fluctuates on his road to *The General Theory,* he was done grappling with this problem. He discovered that when the intended levels of saving and investment are not equal, contraction or expansion of the economy will eventually bring them back into equilibrium.

With this problem solved, Keynes's attention turned to his other concern about the behavior of businessmen: their fear in the face of uncertainty and the low levels of investment that were caused by this fear. In constructing his argument in the *Treatise,* he had been hamstrung not only by his inability to see a solution for the problem of how to balance saving and investment, but also by his "magic formula mentality": he saw changes in the interest rate as the obvious solution and refused to consider seriously that capitalists' fear of an uncertain future might also be jamming the machine. We have only to look to his vehement efforts to dissuade Pigou from exactly this explanation in 1930 in his testimony before the Macmillan Committee to see how blinkered he was by his own mechanistic approach as he was wrapping up the *Treatise*. But once he had fully grasped the importance of the multiplier and used this to help develop his theory of effective demand, he could stop worrying about equating saving with investment and return to his earlier concern with the detrimental effects of uncertainty.

But, of course, as we have seen, as Keynes turned his attention in this direction, he quickly lost his "magic formula mentality." He hoped that it would be possible that public works could be used as a kind of counterweight to stabilize investor expectations. This is a different role from the one that is often associated with his name, for after 1933 he did not endorse government deficits as the means to achieving this end, and he always believed that in the end the solution to this problem of capitalism lay with the behavior of capitalists, not in facilitating a state takeover of the economy. As one would expect from a lifelong Liberal, he found the argument for the role of the state to be complex and nuanced, not blunt and facile. In short, the solution to the problem of maintaining the legitimacy of capitalism was a *moral* problem, not a mechanical one.

Keynes's Relevance Today

So what is Keynes's relevance today, now that concern about another Great Depression has given way to concern about government debt and the level of public spending? We may find his moral critique attractive, but critics argue that Keynes is discredited and that we should be facing up to the fact that his vision of managing the economy to ensure perpetual full employment is a chimera—they have been decisively proved wrong by the events of the past forty years. Government spending and fiscal deficits are the problem, not the solution. Stability is to be achieved through austerity and though dismantling the unaffordable welfare state. This is a return to the attitudes and policies of the 1920s and early 1930s, when the call was for cuts in public spending to restore confidence; so much so that, as late as 1932, in the depths of the Great Depression, even Roosevelt ran on a platform of a balanced budget. This view of policy is backed up by economic theories in which agents are completely rational, they operate in perfect, frictionless markets, and their behavior is dominated by their expectations of the future. In such theories, because markets are assumed to work perfectly, and agents in the private sector are so close to omniscient, it follows almost inexorably that government intervention can only make things worse than if private enterprise were allowed free rein. The world appears to have turned full circle.

If Keynes were the Keynes to which the world turned in the 1960s—if he were the advocate of finely tuning the deficit through changes in tax rates and public spending so as to ensure a high level of aggregate demand and continuous full employment—it would be hard to argue for a return to his theories and policies. The constraints imposed by bond markets and doubts about the ability of governments to implement policy effectively, would make this impossible. So effective have been the libertarian attacks on the confidence—inherited by Keynes from his teachers—that government, for all its faults, could become more efficient, that 1960s Keynesianism is simply not politically feasible.

There is, however, a different Keynes, more attuned to our current concerns. The Keynes we have presented in this book is not the social planner committed to the use of government deficits to maintain the welfare state but an economist who was in many ways skeptical about government, who saw individualist capitalism as essential to freedom, and who could praise Friedrich Hayek's *Road to Serfdom* (1944), the book that for many years has served as the manifesto of free-market economics. He saw that though capitalism was essential, it was flawed and that a way had to be found to cure it of its main defect, namely the failure to stabilize investment. In seeking to maintain investment, and not merely stimulating consumption to compensate for lack of investment, he was taking a long-term view that should be congenial both to those who are concerned about deficits—for there is nothing unsustainable about borrowing to finance productive investment—and to those who are conscious of the need to invest in greener technology.

This, of course, leaves open the question of how Keynesian theories are to be defended against the technical arguments made by his critics. Here, we find a range of responses. The "fundamentalist" response is to turn back to the pages of his *General Theory,* seeking to recover the "true" Keynesian theory. Keynes, the argument runs, recognized that the world was, to use a term that he did not himself use, "non-ergodic," meaning that it does not repeat itself. As a consequence, economic agents face uncertainty that cannot be reduced to measurable probabilities, an argument that, if taken seriously, implies outright rejection of the type of mathematical modeling that has dominated economics since the Second World War. In this view, the theories used to criticize Keynes can simply be rejected as inappropriate to the world in which we live.

A different response is to seek to create new theories, drawing on contemporary economic ideas and methods to create models of why markets fail to generate full employment. Thus Joseph Stiglitz has turned to the concept of asymmetric information—the idea that some people know more than others. His models involve advanced mathematics and rest on highly abstract assumptions, but they have been used to challenge some of the basic intuitions on which free-market theories rest, such as the notion that in a competitive market, price will always adjust so as to make supply equal to demand. The notion that the price of something will rise if demand for it exceeds supply (or will fall if demand is less than supply) may seem obvious, but it may, as Stiglitz has shown, be a very misleading insight. Once this conclusion is accepted, the theoretical objections to Keynesian economics disappear, for there is no smoothly operating alternative to take its place.

Another approach is to turn to what has come to be known as "behavioral economics." This involves using new sources of evidence, such as experiments, to establish how people actually behave in different circumstances. For example, George Akerlof and Robert Shiller have used the methods of behavioral economics to give substance to Keynes's notion of animal spirits, the urge to do something rather than nothing. They have challenged the idea that people are completely rational, providing another route toward Keynesian conclusions.

How should we respond to such different visions of Keynesian economics? The traditional approach has been to search for a way through Keynes's many changes of mind, and the plethora of arguments found in *The General Theory,* to uncover the essential theory. Our approach is different in that rather than seeing the ambiguity and flexibility in Keynes's work as a problem, we see it as the key to understanding him better. Keynes was not trying to lay down a new orthodoxy but was challenging all orthodoxies: he was advocating a perpetual revolution. Clearly, there were certain points to which he was committed, most significantly that the economic system was not self-adjusting because it could not generate the right level of investment; and his belief that government had to take responsibility for managing the economy. There were also specific ideas to which he attached importance. But these were not sufficient to define a unique Keynesian theory, leaving the way open to develop theories that were relevant to new situations.

One barrier to understanding Keynes is the belief that his theory has to be understood as providing a simple formula that will tell us precisely what to do. However, to do this is to adopt the magic formula mentality that Keynes had abandoned by *The General Theory*. He did offer a theory that told governments what needed to be done to get out of the Great Depression, but when circumstances changed, he changed his mind. His analysis of inflation during the Second World War and his plans for a new international economic order after the war certainly reflected the ideas found in *The General Theory* but they went beyond it. There would seem little doubt that, had he lived longer, his thinking would have developed further in response to new circumstances. It was essential not to allow an encrusted orthodoxy to develop. As his Bloomsbury friend Roger Fry put it, "I have always looked on my system with certain suspicion. I have recognised that if it ever formed too solid a crust it might stop the inlets of fresh experience."[5] It is fair to conjecture that he would have been critical of an orthodoxy based on his own work as he was of the orthodoxy defined by much as of the "classical" theory that he attacked in *The General Theory.*

However, perhaps the greatest obstacle to understanding and learning from Keynes is the etiolated ways in which people now talk about capitalism. Advocates of capitalism seem to come only in variants of a similar argument: either you have laissez-faire or you have socialism. It seems almost impossible, in the polarized world in which we live at the beginning of the twenty-first century, for many people to imagine that one could favor capitalism but also believe that it doesn't always function well. In fact, this type of belief is so prevalent that it is difficult to conjure a contemporary advocate of capitalism who is willing to admit that it may need to be regulated or that it could possibly fail to "deliver the goods." This style of uncritical praise for capitalism is especially common in the United States, but it has its supporters in many countries.

Unfortunately, even those on the left who want to retain capitalism but to reform it seem to be unable to generate a more robust argument to counter the "all or nothing" rhetoric of the libertarian right. As Tony Judt says in the quotation earlier in this chapter, the left seems unable to find a compelling rhetoric to explain the need for social democracy. The result was that, once the size of the stimulus packages of 2009 was weighed against the loss of tax revenue caused by the recession, and the huge increase in national debt levels was revealed, the libertarian right quickly attacked the long-run sustainability of the welfare state itself. One waits in vain for the response of the left to these attacks on the modern nation-state: it is as though they cannot believe that people may be asking questions about whether the welfare state needs to be continued. But, if Judt is right, social democrats do need to provide a new and robust defense of their position.

We have argued that Keynes may not be a great place to look for defenses of the welfare state, for the welfare state was not one of his passions. Contrary to what was once widely believed, his writings do not support the running of perpetual deficits, either to stabilize the economy or to finance the welfare state. Keynes does not offer an easy solution (or solutions) to the current crisis. What he does offer, and this is perhaps more important, is a way of seeing beyond the blinkered understanding of capitalism that has prevailed in recent decades. The caricatures of Keynes that abound in public debate match well with the one-dimensional rhetoric that seems to flow from both sides of the political spectrum. In contrast, Keynes's position—that capitalism may be the best system on offer, but that it is beset by internal moral problems and that its legitimacy is threatened by its tendency to instability and high levels of unemployment—is worth taking seriously, if only because it offers a vision of capitalism that transcends the simplistic alternatives on offer. If such an understanding led to new and more nuanced understandings of capitalism's limits and potential, John Maynard Keynes would likely be very pleased. For such an evolution of ideas would represent exactly the kind of perpetual revolution in thinking that he imagined would be necessary as long as capitalism remained a viable system.

DOCUMENTING THE KEYNESIAN REVOLUTION

A Bibliographic Essay

In the opening sentences of the Introduction to his *General Theory of Employment, Interest and Money,* Keynes wrote, "This book is chiefly addressed to my fellow economists. I hope it will be intelligible to others." Our ambition was exactly the opposite. We wrote this book for a general audience, hoping that it would also speak to our fellow economists. As we have tried to make clear, Keynes was initially generous in supporting many different interpreters of his work; and during the last decade of his life he did not try to close down debates over Keynesian economics by offering a definitive interpretation of *The General Theory.* Instead, what developed was a series of orthodoxies initiated by others, each of which claimed title to the mantle of being the true Keynesianism. Thus, following a meeting with economists in Washington in 1944, he remarked that "I found myself the only non-Keynesian there."[1] In developing our account of Keynes, we have clearly benefited from many interpretations of Keynes that capture something important about his work, but we have not cluttered the text with references to other interpretations, preferring to let our interpretation stand on its own. The following essay fills this gap by indicating how our view of Keynes fits with others, thereby acknowledging some of our intellectual debts. Equally important, the fact that the Keynesian revolution was one of the main intellectual events of the twentieth century means that we need to know how Keynes has been interpreted if we are to see the contours of the landscape that was created by his thinking.

Surveying the literature on Keynes is a daunting task. Keynes himself was prolific. He left so much material behind that even though the

Royal Economic Society's edition of his *Collected Writings* runs to thirty volumes, there is still an enormous amount that is not included, some of which is necessary to understand Keynes in his full context. Likewise, the literature on Keynes is immense. It is also very diverse. Most of this literature is concerned not with Keynes as a historical figure but with either co-opting him as a supporter of new ways of doing economics or arguing against them. In this sense, Keynes achieved his desire that many people attempt to work out new systems based on his work. This is why the literature on Keynes is so immense: there is a virtual industry created by the publication of new books and articles about him.

The Primary Literature

Keynes scholars are lucky to have a well-edited, beautifully produced edition of his *Collected Writings.* This edition contains not only the ten books published in his lifetime, but also several important pamphlets and small books, at least one of which, *Two Memoirs,* was published posthumously (1947); as well as newspaper articles, memoranda, letters, and White Papers that he wrote while working in government, book reviews, transcripts of radio broadcasts, voluminous correspondence with all sorts of people, and much else. The inclusion of his correspondence and of the early drafts of *The General Theory* in the *Collected Writings* has been a windfall for historians, making it possible to trace the evolution of his ideas in great detail and producing an enormous secondary literature. A boom in the latter occurred during the late 1970s and 1980s when key documents became more widely available.

Most of the materials not included in the *Collected Writings* are available in the Keynes Papers, deposited at the King's College Modern Archive at Cambridge University, the entire contents of which are also available on microfiche. This archive contains Keynes's correspondence with his wife, Lydia. One volume of these letters, edited by his niece, Polly Hill, and his nephew, Geoffrey Keynes (Hill and Keynes 1990), has been published, but there are enough remaining letters for additional volumes. In a similar vein, Keynes's correspondence from his undergraduate days with his friend Lytton Strachey is not published. These letters contain considerable reflection on Keynes's homosexual interests when he was a young man, including his jejune theory of what the two of them called the "Higher Sodomy."

These parts of Keynes's correspondence are indispensable for a full understanding of his life and work. So are his early correspondence and his undergraduate essays on the philosophy of probability. In fact, some of the correspondence necessary to piecing together the evolution of his early beliefs on probability theory is intertwined in his correspondence with Strachey. But the most important unpublished early writing is a series of essays that he wrote to read to the Apostles on Saturday evenings, the most important of which deal directly with probability or with the questions in moral theory that prompted his interest in probability.

The last work that needs to be included here, though not actually written by Keynes, is the set of student notes from his lectures in 1931–1935, compiled and edited by Thomas Rymes (1989). The notes taken by various students have been merged to create a "representative" set of notes. These are indispensable for tracking the evolution of particular ideas in *The General Theory,* as Keynes often lectured from galley proofs of sections of the book that he paid to have printed. Often the material in these galleys was completely revised in later drafts of the book, but in the absence of photocopying machines Keynes used typesetters and galley proofs as a means to disseminate his ideas widely and to get feedback on them. Many of these early galleys are reproduced in volumes 13 and 14 of the *Collected Writings.*

Biography

Keynes's official biographer was Roy Harrod, whose *Life of John Maynard Keynes* was published in 1951. This was a mere five years after Keynes's death, when *The General Theory* was central to debates over economic theory, and the case for Keynesian policies was still being made. Committed to the Keynesian cause, Harrod's biography was intended to promote the Keynesian revolution by presenting Keynes as a figure who could inspire the new generation. The result was that although he had access to most of the papers (some were not discovered till much later, such as those lost in a laundry basket in Keynes's country home), he was selective in what he used: not only was Keynes's mother still alive, but it would not have served the cause of the Keynesian revolution to reveal his homosexuality (still a crime punishable by imprisonment), his conscientious objection to the First World War, or the extent of his involvement in Bloomsbury. Better to overlook them as youthful indiscretions that had no bearing on the mature Keynes.

Harrod's was the definitive account of Keynes' life for over forty years. This position was not challenged until Robert Skidelsky, a political scientist who had written extensively on the 1930s, turned to Keynes. The first of his three volumes appeared in 1983. Taking the story only up to 1920, this showed the Bloomsbury Keynes, youthful "indiscretions" and all. In volume 2 (1992) he portrayed a mature Keynes for whom Bloomsbury was an integral part of his life. The first complete biography since Harrod's, however, was *Maynard Keynes: An Economist's Biography* (1992), by Donald Moggridge, who had played a major role in editing the *Collected Writings*. The subtitle alluded not just to the biography's being written by an economist, but also to its portrayal of Keynes as an economist. Bloomsbury was important to Keynes, though not the most significant intellectual influence. Moggridge focused on Keynes's continuing involvement in government policy discussions throughout his life, disentangling his role in the Second World War. Skidelsky's volume 3 (2000), interestingly subtitled "Fighting for Britain" in Britain and "Fighting for Freedom" in the United States, completed the life; it was then abridged, in 2003, into the single volume he had originally set out to write.

Keynes scholars have focused much of their attention on the differing interpretations of the biographies by Moggridge and Skidelsky (see, for example, Blaug 1994, Laidler 2002, Moggridge 2002), although there are several other biographies. Keynes's colleague Austin Robinson wrote a long biographical sketch as his obituary for Keynes in the *Economic Journal* in 1947; this outstanding piece captures very clearly Keynes's interest in developing economic theory that could be used to accurately diagnose the economic malfunctions of capitalism in the 1920s and 1930s. In other book-length biographies, Charles Hession (1984) has tried to interpret Keynes's life and work through the lens of what he terms Keynes's "androgyny." The biography by David Felix (1995, 1999) is not about Keynes per se, but rather about *The General Theory;* written as "the biography of an idea," it also fits into another genre, the anti-Keynesian literature that, for all the tribute paid to Keynes's greatness, attempts to criticize and delegitimate his work. More recent introductions to Keynes's life and work include Toye (2000), Dostaler (2007), Cord (2007), and Davidson (2007). In addition there has been a virtual avalanche of journal articles and volumes of papers on Keynes, many of them marking anniversaries, covering subjects ranging from reinterpretations of Keynesian theory to his views on race; the seventieth anniversary of the publication of *The General Theory* alone produced at least six volumes of such work.

Economics

As we explained in Chapter 2, as soon as *The General Theory* appeared, it was the subject of intense discussion. Most of this literature involved using mathematical models to make sense of Keynes's arguments and to relate them to other economic theories (see Young 1987). Most of this literature is of concern only to specialists, though it matters because it laid down what became, by the 1960s, the Keynesian orthodoxy that provides the backdrop to subsequent discussions of Keynes. In this literature, represented by Lawrence Klein's *The Keynesian Revolution* (1947), originally an MIT doctoral dissertation supervised by Paul Samuelson, Keynes was the economist who offered a new theoretical system that could be captured in a simple mathematical model and that offered a way to use changes in government spending and taxation to maintain full employment. If capitalist economies could be cured of this defect, the price mechanism could be left to get on with allocating resources. This was what Samuelson, in the 1955 edition of his best-selling introductory textbook, *Economics* (1955), called "the neoclassical synthesis."

Not everyone accepted this view of Keynes. For example, Sidney Weintraub developed a model that included consideration of income distribution as a key element in the "Keynesian" model. A much more significant critique of neoclassical-synthesis Keynesianism came in another book derived from a Ph.D. dissertation, Axel Leijonhufvud's *On Keynesian Economics and the Economics of Keynes* (1968). His title summarized his thesis: what had come to be thought of as Keynesian economics (Samuelson's neoclassical synthesis) was not the economics to be found in Keynes. The standard view was that Keynesian economics was about what happened when wages were inflexible. As Don Patinkin (1965), another leading figure in establishing the standard view, had put it, Keynesian economics was about what happened when wages did not adjust sufficiently quickly to remove unemployment in a socially acceptable period of time: even if this implied that Keynesian economics was a special case of "classical" economics, it was the special case relevant to the world in which we live.

The problem with the neoclassical-synthesis interpretation, Leijonhufvud claimed, was that Keynes made it clear that the aim of his book was to *deny* that unemployment was caused by wages' being too high. Instead, Leijonhufvud argued, unemployment arose because financial markets failed to establish a rate of interest that would coordinate the decisions of savers and investors. Saving takes place because people want to postpone their spending, and investment is about creating capital resources that will yield income in the future. This means that Keynesian unemployment should be conceived as a failure of intertemporal coordination. Keynesian economics was, as Keynes had claimed, about the general case, in which markets did not have any mechanism to ensure that demand and supply were always in equilibrium with each other. (There are markets in which supply and demand are matched all the time, the obvious example being securities markets, but these are the exceptions that prove the rule, for they are highly centralized and governed by elaborate regulations about how trading takes place.)

At much the same time, Keynesian economics was under attack from free-market economists. Milton Friedman's PBS television series *Free to Choose* (1980)[2] provided a free-market counter to John Kenneth

Galbraith's *The Age of Uncertainty* (1977), a Keynesian series screened three years earlier (both series were turned into best-selling books). But though Friedman was the most prominent publicist for free markets, it was James Buchanan who provided the most comprehensive reexamination of Keynes, in his *Democracy in Deficit: The Political Legacy of Lord Keynes* (1977). He described Keynes as a supporter of deficit spending who helped to undermine what he called our "fiscal constitution," according to which governments should balance their budgets except in time of war. In removing this constraint on irresponsible government behavior, Keynes had unleashed the inflationary turmoil of the 1970s.

The 1970s also saw the creation of a group who called themselves "Post-Keynesians." This was not the first time the term had been used; the early Keynesians had appropriated the term in the 1950s; but it was the first time it was used to denote an organized movement rebelling against the discipline's orthodoxy. Its leaders were Joan Robinson, one of the young Keynesians who had worked alongside Keynes in the 1930s and been one of the first popularizers of *The General Theory* in 1936; Paul Davidson, a student of Sidney Weintraub's; and some young economists inspired by their work. Their motivation was twofold: they objected to the technical requirements being imposed by the most important academic journals, which meant that their work—less formal and, as they saw it, more realistic—was excluded; and they objected to the move away from full-employment policies. Turning to parts of *The General Theory* that they believed had been unduly neglected, they emphasized that it was concerned with a world in which time and uncertainty played crucial roles, rendering the techniques used by orthodox "neoclassical" economists inappropriate. What was needed was, to quote the title of a book by Jan Kregel, one of those who appropriated the label "Post-Keynesian" to describe the new movement, *A Reconstruction of Economic Theory* (1973). They came to be known by some as "fundamentalist" Keynesians. Post-Keynesians' accounts of their history, notably that of John King (2002), start from *The General Theory*, but it is an identity that dates only from the 1970s. At the same time, George Shackle (1973) was grounding Keynes's views of uncertainty on limitations of human knowledge that, he argued, were a consequence of the irreversibility of time; and Hyman Minsky (1976) proposed an interpretation of Keynes that placed even more emphasis on the instability of modern finance. One of Minsky's students, who became a leading Post-Keynesian, Victoria Chick (1983), offered an interpretation of *The General Theory* as comprising many layers: at one level there was the IS-LM model, but as layers were peeled away there emerged a theory in which time and uncertainty played a bigger role. Though both Shackle and Minsky put forward ideas that were congenial to Post-Keynesians, who drew on their ideas, they retained highly distinctive positions.

One of the most significant interpreters of Keynes in the 1970s was Harry Johnson, a Chicago-trained economist with a high profile in the profession. His interest in the sociology of the economics profession led him to novel reinterpretations of the Keynesian revolution and of Keynes in relation to Cambridge. His work was brought together with essays on Keynes by his wife Elizabeth Johnson, one of the editors of Keynes's *Collected Writings*, in *The Shadow of Keynes* (1977).

During the 1970s, other economists approached Keynes with more historical purposes. A major stimulus was the publication of key volumes in the *Collected Writings*, documenting the process whereby Keynes wrote *The General Theory*. Patinkin (1976, 1982) used these to produce a reevaluation of Keynes's monetary thought, and tried to settle the still-unresolved question of whether Keynes's ideas had been anticipated by Swedish and Polish economists. (His conclusion was no, on the grounds that their theories did not have what he believed were the three essential features of *The General Theory:* the multiplier, quantity adjustments, and unemployment equilibrium.) A decade later, when a monetarist, Allan Meltzer (1988), challenged the prevailing view of Keynes by claiming that he had the more limited objective of stabilizing private investment at a higher level than would happen if the government did nothing, Patinkin (1990) took up the challenge. He countered that Meltzer was wrong to depict Keynes as focused on the potential for private investment to stabilize the economy, for Keynes was primarily interested in the use of fiscal policy to eradicate unemployment. A central point in their dispute was whether the final chapter of *The General Theory,* titled "Concluding Notes on the Social Philosophy toward Which the General Theory Might Lead," was, as its title might suggest, an afterthought, or whether it had formed part of what Patinkin called the book's "central message" about the efficacy of fiscal policy. If this chapter did represent Keynes's central message, then Meltzer would be more correct than Patinkin, for it barely mentions fiscal policy, and policies to stabilize private-sector investment take center stage. Patinkin could keep alive the old vision of *The General Theory*'s being about using fiscal policy to achieve continuous full employment only by arguing that the chapter was peripheral to Keynes's argument. It is not clear that his argument was persuasive to anyone who did not already share his view.

More recently, after the transformation in macroeconomics wrought by the New Classical economists and their successors, the Keynesian revolution has come to be seen through the lens of the New Keynesian economics, in which wage stickiness is seen as the cause of unemployment. Examples include Michael Woodford (1999) and Olivier Blanchard (2000). The effort to resurrect Keynesian economics on the foundation of sticky wages is no small irony, given that Keynes's writings in the 1930s were largely meant to find a way to move beyond theories of wage stickiness as an explanation of mass unemployment.

Philosophy and History

From the 1970s, when Keynes's ideas became unfashionable among economists and policymakers, there was increased interest in placing Keynes's work in its full historical context. This was stimulated both by the appearance of his *Collected Writings* and by the changing status of his work, for as substantive criticisms of orthodox Keynesianism mounted, people began to question the extent to which these critiques addressed what Keynes had actually said.

During the 1970s and 1980s, one of the main arguments made in the anti-Keynesian literature was that Keynes and his followers had failed to understand how much people's expectations of the future influenced their behavior. His critics argued, for instance, that he had not understood that people would change their expectations of the future when the government changed its policies and that these changes helped explain the supposed failure of Keynesian policy to successfully address the stagflation of the 1970s. For anyone familiar with *The General Theory,* this was a remarkable claim, since Keynes wrote extensively there about expectations.

The concern by some Keynesian scholars to better understand Keynes's views of uncertainty and expectations led to the first serious efforts to examine his economics in light of his earlier interest in the philosophy of probability, in particular the work that had led to his *Treatise on Probability* (1921, JMK 8). A key interpretative problem, addressed in three Ph.D. dissertations completed in the 1980s and in the subsequent literature, involved the question of whether Keynes had meant what he said in his response to the philosopher Frank Ramsey's (1931) criticism of his work on probability, after Ramsey's death.[3] Ramsey had been a close acquaintance of Keynes's, and Keynes appeared to be accepting Ramsey's criticism that the objective logical relations upon which Keynes had based his *Treatise on Probability* simply did not exist. Anna Carabelli (1988) argued that Keynes had never held an objective theory of probability, and so never changed his mind. Roderick O'Donnell (1989) argued that Keynes never seriously accepted Ramsey's criticism. In contrast, Bradley Bateman (1987, 1988, 1996) accepted that Keynes had accepted Ramsey's criticism and tried to show how this change helped to explain why expectations had played little or no role in Keynes's *Tract on Monetary Reform* (1923) or his *Treatise on Money* (1930), but had become central in *The General Theory* (1936).

Other interpretations of the influence of Keynes's early work in philosophy on his later work in economics include John Davis (1994), who tried to place Keynes's work in the wider framework of Cambridge philosophy in the early twentieth century, and Donald Gillies and Grazia Ietto-Gillies (1991), who explained how Keynes built on Ramsey's work to develop an intersubjective theory of probability (a theory in which probability depends on the beliefs of a community rather than those of individuals) in his later economics. Mizuhara and Runde (2003) contains retrospective views of the subject by many of these authors and others who took up these ideas. Backhouse and Bateman's *Cambridge Companion to Keynes* (2006) treats this topic as part of a more general survey of the philosophical influences on Keynes's work, ranging from his interests in ethics and probability to his participation in Bloomsbury, set against the background of his economics.

A parallel literature looked more closely at how Keynesian ideas had originally spread across the industrial democracies. One aspect of this was the spread of Keynesian ideas in Britain, work on this being stimulated by the reduction from fifty to thirty years in the period for which British government archives were closed to scholars. Written almost exclusively by economic historians, this literature examined the extent to which Keynes's ideas had penetrated into the policymaking process in Britain and the ways in which politicians and civil servants reacted to his ideas. Among the first historians to do this were Susan Howson and Donald Winch (1977), followed, in the 1980s, by a spate of writing by young economic historians, much of which is surveyed by George Peden (1988). Peden (2004) reproduces key government documents that bear on the issues in this debate.

Peter Hall (1989) painted a much broader picture in a volume containing essays by historians, political scientists, economists, and sociologists that examine the transmission of Keynesian ideas from one country to another. Hall reached the awkward conclusion, consistent with the story of the slow spread of Keynesianism in British official circles, that the initial adoption of "Keynesian" policies had very little to do with Keynes. In virtually all industrial democracies, the introduction of fiscal policy to stabilize the economy was the result of political innovation by people who knew nothing of Keynes's ideas.

The question of what Keynes's own political beliefs were and how they informed his economics is the subject of yet another literature. Michael Freeden (1978) first examined the question of whether Keynes was a "New Liberal," part of the stream of more collectivist liberalism that emerged in Britain in the decades around 1900; this movement honored the traditional autonomy of the individual while asking what the state's role might be in securing the welfare of the individual given the dramatic changes in fortunes dictated by mass production and industrial society.

Peter Clarke's (1978) examination of New Liberalism led him, like Freeden, to Keynes and ultimately to a full historical account of the evolution of Keynes's ideas. To this historian, much of the literature on Keynes seemed to paint a picture of a "composite Aunt Sally of uncertain age"—a phrase first used by Dennis Robertson to describe Keynes's characterization of classical economics.[4] His exploration of Keynes's simultaneous work on economic theory and as an advisor to the government on economic policy led to his comprehensive study (1988) of exactly when (and how) Keynes made his most important breakthroughs. The book marked a new standard in historical scholarship on Keynes's ideas. Clarke was, of course, not the only scholar to use the newly available material to reinterpret Keynes. Robert Dimand (1988) offered an interpretation of the Keynesian revolution, like Patinkin and Meltzer from an economist's perspective, though attaching more importance than was customary to the *Treatise on Money.* A decade after that, David Laidler redrew the picture of the interwar macroeconomic landscape, changing our perspective not so much by offering new evidence on Keynes as by transforming our understanding of what Keynes had dismissed as "classical economics," provocatively calling his book *Fabricating the Keynesian Revolution* (1999): in his account, on which we draw heavily, there was a Keynesian revolution, but it involved building on what had gone before, not sweeping it away. In a more recent essay, Backhouse and Laidler (2004) have filled out this picture by pointing to what was lost as well as gained in the Keynesian revolution.

Throughout his career, Keynes was concerned with international monetary problems and hence with international relations. Donald Markwell (2006) has traced an evolution of Keynes's thinking. He started with classical liberal views on the relationship between free trade and peace. In the interwar period he argued that international cooperation was needed to restart the European economies, but in the 1930s came to call for a degree of national self-sufficiency. His work toward the post–Second World War settlement represents the mature phase of his thinking, characterized by Markwell as liberal institutionalism: full employment and new international monetary institutions would eliminate the economic causes of war and permit a peaceful regime of free trade.

Keynes after the Crisis

The upsurge of interest in Keynes after the financial crisis has resulted in a flurry of short books on Keynes and Keynesian economics. At one end of the spectrum are books that, though they cover Keynes in order to revive Keynesian economics, are primarily economists' analyses of the crisis that, though not advancing our understanding of the historical Keynes, make fresh cases for the relevance of his work. These authors are mostly economists for whom the crisis confirmed long-held views, whether those views were orthodox (Krugman 2008) or heterodox Keynesianism (Davidson 2009). George Akerlof and Robert Shiller (2009) use insights from behavioral finance (including results derived from experimental techniques not available to economists writing even a decade earlier) to revive a version of Keynes's notion of "animal spirits," the spontaneous urge to do something rather than nothing. An exception is Richard Posner (2009), a self-confessed conservative, eminent in the field of law and economics, for whom the failure of capitalism revealed by the crisis of 2008 provided a reason to reappraise Keynesian economics.

Alongside such works are books by Keynes scholars. Skidelsky had, in 1996, produced a short book, titled simply *Keynes,* arguing that Keynes "had joined Marx as the God that failed."[5] The reason, Skidelsky contended, was that Keynes's followers had been too ambitious, bringing about the inflation and economic instability of the 1970s. In contrast, after the crisis, Skidelsky found Keynes to be relevant once more. Skidelsky's *Keynes: The Return of the Master* (2009) draws on the immense scholarship that lies behind his three-volume biography in providing a vignette of Keynes's life, including an account of his activities as an investor. Much of the book, however, offers a diagnosis of the crisis, presenting Keynesian economics as the basis on which economics can be reconstructed. From the "Bloomsbury Keynes" of volume 1 of his trilogy (1983), Skidelsky has moved to a Post-Keynesian perspective according to which radical uncertainty (uncertainty that cannot be modeled using numerical probabilities) undermines all orthodox economics. In contrast, although Clarke clearly believes that Keynes's ideas are extremely important, his *Keynes: The Twentieth Century's Greatest Economist* (2009) focuses on Keynes's life and work, retaining the historian's distance from his subject.

In writing this book, we were influenced, whether positively or negatively, consciously or unconsciously, by all the literature discussed here, and by much that space constraints have not allowed us to mention. Our emphasis on the importance of Keynes's vision of capitalism as a complex, evolving system is closest to Clarke's view of Keynes, though we have drawn extensively on the two major biographies. Moggridge was particularly valuable in detailing Keynes's policy involvements in both peace and war. In emphasizing the importance of Bloomsbury we are following the examples of Skidelsky (1983) and later Goodwin (1998, 2006). It is to Goodwin that we owe the key insight concerning the Bloomsbury roots of Keynes's flexibility and his resistance to orthodoxy, whether that of his predecessors or of an orthodoxy that might be built on his own work. Our understanding of the Keynesian revolution has been shaped by the work of Hall on the spread of Keynesianism, and that of Laidler on the relationship of *The General Theory* to the monetary economics of the interwar period.

NOTES

The abbreviation JMK refers to *The Collected Writings of John Maynard Keynes.*

1. Keynes Returns, but Which Keynes?

1. JMK 7:149–150.
2. Ibid., pp. 154–155.
3. Ibid., p. 159.
4. Ibid., p. 160.
5. Ibid., pp. xxiii, 16.

2. The Rise and Fall of Keynesian Economics

1. JMK 13:395.
2. Laidler 1999:3.
3. James 1989:234.
4. Samuelson 1944:298.
5. Schumpeter 1954:1176.
6. Interview with Robert J. Barro in Snowdon, Vane, and Wynarczyk 1994:269.
7. Lucas and Sargent 1978:49–50.

3. Keynes the Moral Philosopher

1. Webb and Webb 1935.
2. JMK 9:292.
3. JMK 17:450.
4. JMK 9:293.
5. JMK 28:36.

6. JMK 2:1.
7. Ibid., p. 11.
8. Ibid., p. 12.
9. JMK 4:24.
10. JMK 9:267.
11. Ibid., p. 268.
12. Ibid., p. 57.
13. Ibid., p. 58.
14. JMK 17:269.
15. JMK 19:60.
16. JMK 16:427; cf. JMK 2:179.
17. JMK 18:178.
18. JMK 21:239.
19. Ibid.
20. Cf. JMK 6:135–143.
21. JMK 5:246.
22. Robertson 1915, 1926.
23. JMK 11:342.
24. JMK 17:450.
25. Keynes papers A/2/6.
26. JMK 27:385, 386.
27. Hayek 1944:97.
28. JMK 27:350.
29. JMK 21:239–240.
30. Ibid., p. 90.
31. JMK 28:344.
32. JMK 9:268.
33. Ibid., p. 329.
34. Ibid.
35. Ibid.
36. Ibid., chapter 24.
37. JMK 7:374–382; 9:325; 13:491.
38. JMK 13:491.
39. JMK 7:221, 375.
40. JMK 9:328.

41. See Goodwin 1998, 2006.
42. Goodwin 2006:224.
43. Ibid., quoting JMK 9:327.

4. Keynes the Physician

1. JMK 14:36.
2. Ibid.
3. Letter from Keynes to his mother dated 14 September 1930 in JMK 13:176.
4. HMSO 1931, *QQ 6613-16.*
5. Patinkin 1976:53, 126.
6. JMK 14:121–122.
7. See Clarke 2009:148.
8. Henderson to Keynes, February 28, 1933, in JMK 21:166.
9. JMK 7:378.
10. JMK 13:548; quoted in Clarke 2009:151.
11. JMK 7:377.
12. JMK 27:326.
13. Ibid., p. 353; quoted in Moggridge 1992:712.
14. JMK 27:406.
15. JMK 23:191.
16. JMK 14:108–123.

5. Keynes's Ambiguous Revolution

1. JMK 7:3.
2. Pigou 1936:115.
3. JMK 14:121.
4. Ibid., p. 122.
5. JMK 7:380.
6. JMK 27:443.
7. JMK 14:79.
8. Colander 1984.
9. Moggridge 1986:361.

10. Harrod 1937:85; JMK 14:84; cf. Moggridge 1986:361.

11. Hayek 1995:232.

12. Backhouse 2010:133.

13. Skidelsky 1992:539.

14. Rymes 1989:102.

15. Ibid.

16. JMK 7:297–298.

17. JMK 14:150.

18. JMK 7:155.

19. Ibid., p. 376.

20. Goodwin 2006:221.

21. Goodwin 1998:76.

22. JMK 14:259.

23. Goodwin 1998:198.

6. Perpetual Revolution

1. MacKenzie 2006:150.

2. Judt 2010:34. This is an elaboration of an argument summarized in Judt 2009.

3. JMK 9:287.

4. Ibid., p. 291.

5. Quoted in Goodwin 2006:235.

Documenting the Keynesian Revolution

1. Robinson 1972:541–542.

2. Friedman and Friedman 1980.

3. JMK 10:336–339.

4. Robertson 1937:436.

5. Skidelsky 1996:107.

REFERENCES

Akerlof, George A., and Robert Shiller. 2009. *Animal Spirits: How Human Psychology Drives the Economy and Why It Matters for Global Capitalism.* Princeton: Princeton University Press.

Backhouse, Roger E. 2010. "'An Abstruse and Mathematical Argument': The Use of Mathematical Reasoning in the General Theory." In *The Return to Keynes: Keynes and Keynesian Policies in the New Millennium,* ed. Bradley W. Bateman, Cristina Marcuzzo, and Tokiashi Hirai. Cambridge, Mass.: Harvard University Press.

Backhouse, Roger E., and Bradley W. Bateman, eds. 2006. *The Cambridge Companion to Keynes.* Cambridge: Cambridge University Press.

Backhouse, Roger E., and Bradley W. Bateman. 2010. "Whose Keynes?" In *Keynes's General Theory: A Reconsideration after Seventy Years,* ed. R. W. Dimand, R. Mundell, and A. Vercelli. London: Palgrave for the International Economic Association.

Backhouse, Roger E., and David E. W. Laidler. 2004. "What Was Lost with IS-LM?" *History of Political Economy* 36 (annual suppl.), *The IS-LM Model: Its Rise, Fall, and Strange Persistence,* ed. K. D. Hoover and M. De Vroey, pp. 25–56.

Bateman, Bradley W. 1987. "Keynes's Changing Conception of Probability." *Economics and Philosophy* 3:97–120.

———. 1988. "G. E. Moore and J. M. Keynes: A Missing Chapter in the History of the Expected Utility Model." *American Economic Review* 78(5): 1098–1106.

———. 1996. *Keynes's Uncertain Revolution.* Ann Arbor: University of Michigan Press.

———. 2010. "Keynes Returns to America." In *The Return to Keynes: Keynes and Keynesian Policies in the New Millennium,* ed. Bradley W. Bateman, Cristina Marcuzzo, and Toshiaki Hirai. Cambridge, Mass.: Harvard University Press.

Bateman, Bradley W., Cristina Marcuzzo, and Toshiaki Hirai, eds. 2010. *The Return to Keynes: Keynes and Keynesian Policies in the New Millennium.* Cambridge, Mass.: Harvard University Press.

Blanchard, Olivier. 2000. "What Do We Know about Macroeconomics That Fisher and Wicksell Did Not?" *Quarterly Journal of Economics* 115(4): 1375–1409.

Blaug, Mark. 1990. *John Maynard Keynes: Life, Ideas, Legacy.* London: Macmillan.

———. 1994. "Recent Biographies of Keynes." *Journal of Economic Literature* 32(3): 1204–1215.

Buchanan, James, and Richard Wagner. 1977. *Democracy in Deficit: The Political Legacy of Lord Keynes.* New York: Academic Press.

Carabelli, Anna M. 1988. *On Keynes's Method.* London: Macmillan.

Chick, Victoria. 1983. *Macroeconomics after Keynes: A Reconsideration of the General Theory.* Cambridge, Mass.: MIT Press.

Clarke, Peter. 1978. *Liberals and Social Democrats.* Cambridge: Cambridge University Press.

———. 1988. *The Keynesian Revolution in the Making, 1924–1936.* Oxford: Clarendon Press.

———. 2009. *Keynes: The Twentieth Century's Most Influential Economist.* London: Bloomsbury.

Colander, David. 1984. "Was Keynes a Keynesian or a Lernerian?" *Journal of Economic Literature* 22:1272–1275.

Cord, Robert. 2007. *Keynes (Life and Times).* London: Haus Publishing.

Davidson, Paul A. 2007. *John Maynard Keynes.* London: Palgrave.

———. 2009. *The Keynes Solution: The Path to Global Economic Prosperity.* London: Palgrave.

Davis, John B. 1994. *Keynes's Philosophical Development.* Cambridge: Cambridge University Press.

Dimand, Robert W. 1988. *The Origins of the Keynesian Revolution: The Development of Keynes's Theory of Employment and Output.* Aldershot: Edward Elgar.

Dostaler, Gilles. 2007. *Keynes and His Battles.* Cheltenham: Edward Elgar.

Felix, David. 1995. *John Maynard Keynes and the General Theory: Biography of an Idea.* New Brunswick, N.J.: Transaction.

———. 1999. *Keynes: A Critical Life.* Westport, Conn.: Greenwood Press.

Freeden, Michael. 1978. *The New Liberalism.* Oxford: Oxford University Press.

Friedman, Milton. 1962. *Capitalism and Freedom.* Chicago: Chicago University Press.

Friedman, Milton, and Rose Friedman. 1980. *Free to Choose: A Personal Statement.* New York: Houghton Mifflin.

Galbraith, John Kenneth. 1977. *The Age of Uncertainty.* New York: Houghton Mifflin.

Gillies, Donald, and Grazia Ietto-Gillies. 1991. "Intersubjective Probability and Economics." *Review of Political Economy* 3(4): 393–417.

Goodwin, C. D. W. 1998. *Art and the Market: Roger Fry on Commerce and Art.* Ann Arbor: University of Michigan Press.

———. 2006. *The Art of an Ethical Life: Keynes and Bloomsbury,* ed. R. E. Backhouse and B. W. Bateman. Cambridge: Cambridge University Press.

Hall, Peter, ed. 1989. *The Political Power of Economic Ideas: Keynesianism across Nations.* Princeton: Princeton University Press.

Hansen, Alvin H. 1953. *A Guide to Keynes.* New York: McGraw-Hill.

Harrod, Roy Forbes. 1937. "Mr. Keynes and Traditional Theory." *Econometrica* 5(1): 74–86.

———. 1951. *The Life of John Maynard Keynes.* London: Macmillan.

Hayek, Friedrich A. 1944. *The Road to Serfdom.* London: Routledge.

———. 1995. *Contra Keynes and Cambridge,* ed. Stephen Kresge. London: Routledge.

Hession, Charles H. 1984. *John Maynard Keynes: A Personal Biography of the Man Who Revolutionized Capitalism and the Way We Live.* London: Collier Macmillan.

Hill, Polly, and Richard Keynes. 1990. *Lydia and Maynard: Letters of Lydia Lopokova and John Maynard Keynes.* New York: Scribner.

HMSO. 1931. Committee on Finance and Industry. *Minutes of Evidence*, 2 volumes.

Howson, Susan, and Donald Winch. 1977. *The Economic Advisory Council, 1930–1939: A Study in Economic Advice during Depression and Recovery*. Cambridge: Cambridge University Press.

James, Harold. 1989. "What Is Keynesian about Deficit Financing? The Case of Interwar Germany." In *The Political Power of Economic Ideas: Keynesianism across Nations*, ed. P. A. Hall. Princeton: Princeton University Press.

JMK. See Keynes, John Maynard.

Johnson, Elizabeth, and Harry G. Johnson. 1977. *The Shadow of Keynes*. Chicago: University of Chicago Press.

Judt, Tony. 2009. "What Is Living and What Is Dead in Social Democracy?" *New York Review of Books*, April 29, 2010.

———. 2010. *Ill Fares the Land: A Treatise on Our Present Discontents*. London: Allen Lane.

Keynes, John Maynard. 1971–1989. *The Collected Writings of John Maynard Keynes* (cited as JMK with volume number), ed. Sir Austin Robinson and Donald Moggridge. 30 vols. London: Macmillan.

King, John E. 2002. *A History of Post Keynesian Economics*. Cheltenham: Edward Elgar.

Klein, Lawrence R. 1947. *The Keynesian Revolution*. London: Macmillan.

Kregel, Jan A. 1973. *A Reconstruction of Economic Theory: An Introduction to Post Keynesian Economics*. London: Macmillan.

Krugman, Paul. 2008. *The Return of Depression Economics and the Crisis of 2008*. London: Penguin Books.

Laidler, David E. W. 1999. *Fabricating the Keynesian Revolution: Studies of the Inter-War Literature on Money, the Cycle, and Unemployment*. Cambridge: Cambridge University Press.

———. 2002. "Skidelsky's Keynes: A Review Essay." *European Journal of the History of Economic Thought* 9(1): 97–110.

Leijonhufvud, Axel. 1968. *On Keynesian Economics and the Economics of Keynes*. Oxford: Oxford University Press.

Liberal Industrial Inquiry. 1928. *Britain's Industrial Future: Being the Report of the Liberal Industrial Inquiry.* London: Ernest Benn.

Lucas, Robert E., and Thomas J. Sargent. 1978. "After Keynesian Macroeconomics." In *After the Phillips Curve: Persistence of High Inflation and High Unemployment.* Boston: Federal Reserve Bank of Boston.

MacKenzie, Donald. 2006. *An Engine Not a Camera: How Financial Models Shape Markets.* Cambridge, Mass.: MIT Press.

Markwell, Donald. 2006. *John Maynard Keynes and International Relations: Economic Paths to War and Peace.* Oxford: Oxford University Press.

Meltzer, Allan. 1988. *Keynes's Monetary Theory: A Different Interpretation.* Cambridge: Cambridge University Press.

Minsky, Hyman P. 1976. *John Maynard Keynes.* London: Macmillan.

Mizuhara, Sohei, and Jochen Runde. 2003. *The Philosophy of Keynes's Economics: Probability, Uncertainty and Convention.* London: Routledge.

Moggridge, Donald E. 1986. "Keynes and His Revolution in Historical Perspective." *Eastern Economic Journal* 12(4): 357–369.

———. 1992. *Maynard Keynes: An Economist's Biography.* London: Routltdege.

———. 2002. "Rescuing Keynes from the Economists? The Skidelsky Trilogy." *European Journal of the History of Economic Thought* 9(1): 111–123.

O'Donnell, Roderick. 1989. *Keynes's Philosophy, Economics and Politics: The Philosophical Foundations of Keynes's Thought and Their Influence on His Economics and Politics.* London: Palgrave Macmillan.

Patinkin, Don. 1965. *Money, Interest and Prices.* New York: Harper and Row.

———. 1976. *Keynes's Monetary Thought: A Study of Its Development.* Durham, N.C.: Duke University Press.

———. 1982. *Anticipations of the General Theory and Other Essays on Keynes.* Chicago: University of Chicago Press.

———. 1990. "On Different Interpretations of the *General Theory.*" *Journal of Monetary Economics* 26:205–243.

Peden, George C. 1988. *Keynes, the Treasury, and British Economic Policy.* London: Macmillan Educational.

———. 2004. *Keynes and His Critics: Treasury Responses to the Keynesian Revolution, 1925–1946.* Oxford: Oxford University Press.

Pigou, A. C. 1936. "Mr. J. M. Keynes' General Theory of Employment, Interest and Money." *Economica* N.S. 3(10): 115–132.

Posner, Richard A. 2009. *A Failure of Capitalism: The Crisis of '08 and the Descent into Depression.* Cambridge, Mass.: Harvard University Press.

Ramsey, Frank P. 1931. *Foundations of Mathematics.* London: Kegan Paul.

Robertson, Dennis Holme. 1915. *A Study of Industrial Fluctuation: An Enquiry into the Character and Causes of the So-Called Cyclical Movements of Trade.* London: P. S. King and Son.

———. 1926. *Banking Policy and the Price Level.* London: P. S. King and Son.

———. 1937. "Alternative Theories of the Rate of Interest: Rejoinder." *Economic Journal* 47(187): 428–436.

Robinson, E. A. G. R. 1947. "John Maynard Keynes, 1883–1946." *Economic Journal* 57(225): 1–68.

———. 1972. "John Maynard Keynes: Economist, Author, Statesman." *Economic Journal* 82:531–546.

Rymes, Thomas K., ed. 1989. *Keynes's Lectures, 1932–35: Notes of a Representative Student.* London: Macmillan.

Samuelson, Paul A. 1944. "Unemployment Ahead." *New Republic* 111:297–299.

———. 1955. *Economics*, 3rd ed. New York: McGraw Hill.

Schumpeter, Joseph Alois. 1954. *A History of Modern Economic Analysis.* New York: Oxford University Press.

Shackle, George L. S. 1973. *Epistemics and Economics: A Critique of Economic Doctrines.* Cambridge: Cambridge University Press.

Skidelsky, Robert. 1983. *John Maynard Keynes.* Vol. 1: *Hopes Betrayed, 1883–1920.* London: Macmillan.

———. 1992. *John Maynard Keynes.* Vol. 2: *The Economist as Saviour, 1920–1937.* London: Macmillan.

———. 1996. *Keynes.* Oxford: Oxford University Press.

———. 2000. *John Maynard Keynes.* Vol. 3: *Fighting for Britain, 1937–1946.* London: Macmillan.

———. 2003. *John Maynard Keynes, 1883–1946: Economist, Philosopher, Statesman.* London: Macmillan.

———. 2009. *Keynes: The Return of the Master.* London: Allen Lane.

Toye, John. 2000. *Keynes on Population.* Oxford: Oxford University Press.

Webb, Sidney, and Beatrice Webb. 1935. *Soviet Communism: A New Civilization?* London: Longmans Green.

Woodford, Michael. 1999. "Revolution and Evolution in Macroeconomics." Online at http://www.columbia.edu/%7Emw2230/macro20C.pdf.

Young, Warren. 1987. *Interpreting Mr. Keynes: The IS-LM Enigma.* London: Polity Press.

ACKNOWLEDGMENTS

We began to work together on Keynes when we were invited to edit *The Cambridge Companion to Keynes,* a collection of a dozen essays surveying the current state of knowledge about Keynes. When the book was published, in 2006, we decided there were further things that needed to be said, and we developed some of these ideas in articles and in contributions to other volumes. When the financial crisis erupted, in 2008, we realized that some of these ideas, centered on how Keynes saw capitalism, were of greater relevance than we had dared believe when we started thinking about them. Our sense of the relevance of these ideas has only grown as we have observed how the fiscal stimulus packages of 2009 have led to attacks on the welfare state and stabilization policy. So we conceived the idea of trying to develop them into a short book that could be accessible to people who have no formal training in economics. This book is the result.

Most of these appeared under our joint names, the most significant ones being "Keynes and Capitalism," *History of Political Economy* 41(4): 645–671; and "Whose Keynes?" in *Keynes's General Theory after Seventy Years,* ed. Robert W. Dimand, Robert Mundell, and Alessandro Vercelli (London: International Economic Association/Palgrave Macmillan, 2010. Reproduced with permission of Palgrave Macmillan).

Two pieces appeared under merely one name, although in both cases we had discussed the work extensively before publication: "Keynes Returns to America" (Bateman) and "'An Abstruse and Mathematical Argument': The Use of Mathematical Reasoning in the General Theory" (Backhouse), both appearing in Bradley W. Bateman, Cristina

Marcuzzo, and Tokiashi Hirai, eds., *The Return of Keynes: Keynes and Keynesian Policies in the New Millennium* (Cambridge, Mass.: Harvard University Press, 2010). Ideas from these pieces are used here, and although the material has been completely rewritten several times, some of the original wording no doubt remains. We are grateful to the publishers, Duke University Press, the International Economic Association, and Harvard University Press, for permission to use this material here. Unpublished writings of J. M. Keynes copyright The Provost and Scholars of King's College Cambridge, 2011.

We have chosen not to clutter the text with references to the literature. Instead, a bibliographic essay, "Documenting the Keynesian Revolution," reviews the literature on Keynes, indicating where many of our ideas come from, and explains how our work relates to what has been done before.

We are also extremely grateful to the colleagues who have read material at various stages and whose wisdom and knowledge have saved us from error and provided us with ideas. These include Craufurd Goodwin, David Laidler, Perry Mehrling, Richard Posner, Donald Winch, and two anonymous readers.

INDEX

Note: Authors' names appear after publications written by people other than Keynes; dates appear after publications by Keynes.